BLUE IN CHICAGO

Also by Bette Howland

W-3

BLUE IN CHICAGO

BETTE HOWLAND

Harper & Row, Publishers
New York, Hagerstown, San Francisco, London

"Blue in Chicago," "Golden Age," "Public Facilities," and "To the Country" originally appeared in *Commentary*.

Designed by Ginger Giles

Library of Congress Cataloging in Publication Data
Howland, Bette.
  Blue in Chicago.
  I. Title.
PZ4.H85968Bl   [PS3558.0927]   813'.5'4   76-26235
ISBN 0-06-011957-8

78 79 80 10 9 8 7 6 5 4 3 2

SARAH BERGER
Buc—, Romania   Chicago, Illinois
1889–1975
A hard act to follow

CONTENTS

BLUE
IN CHICAGO

First thing this morning, getting ready to leave the house, I heard on the news report that another University of Chicago graduate student had been shot and killed in a holdup in Hyde Park. I was holding my breath, but the name was not one I knew. I'm a graduate student at the university and I live in Hyde Park. I listened for details—the time of night, a number, a street. You always want to know how close these things have come to you.

There were two students. They were at a party and had gone out to get more beer. On the way back three youths wanted their money. One gave up his wallet and walked away. The other was a black belt in karate—he put up a fight. Five times the gun clicked and misfired; the sixth tore his side. The radio announcer went on to recall other such incidents in the college community, the last student murder only a few months before.

It was a dense dark morning. I live in a small studio on top of a high rise; it's mostly windows. A friend calls it a perch on a flagpole because I never draw the shades. Lately one visitor after another has expressed a wish for an apartment just like mine: "It's perfect," they say. From which I infer that they all want to climb up the flagpole; remove themselves. And there is something remote about my situation. For instance, I can see the helicopters surveying the morning traffic snarls, hovering over the city. On days like today they seem to be putt-putting about in thick gray gloom like outboard motors. The noise takes up the whole sky. Maybe because the details weren't more specific—because the victim was unknown, faceless to me—because I couldn't pinpoint the spot—all at once there were no limits. It was out there: I didn't have to know *where.*

One other thing. I was about to set off for a cousin's wedding, clear on the other side of the city. That's where all my relatives live. And it seems that every time I trek north for one of these family occasions (none of them would dream of going to see me), the subject is bound to come up: why I continue to live on the South Side of Chicago, with its high crime rate and race warfare. Almost inevitably something like this will have happened, played up on the news, plastered all over the headlines. Crime on the South Side gets the banner treatment. Everyone likes to know *where*, to isolate the symptoms. Only this morning I had a strange, obstinate reaction: I didn't feel like being hassled in this way, didn't feel apologetic about living in Hyde Park. Maybe it was just inertia. Or mulishness —a family trait.

My Uncle Rudy's height and hulking shoulders filled the space behind the wheel. A huge man, six foot four, two hundred and fifty pounds; crew-cut, bullet-headed; the thick close-shaven folds of skin lay on his neck. Even from the back, in his checked gray suit, you could tell: a cop. I looked at the back of his head, wondering what he was thinking. Impenetrable. His head seems too small for the big body; his nose is a beak. When his nose got broken somehow, on maneuvers, the army doctors wanted to make it over for him. But Rudy wouldn't hear of it. Why kibitz with destiny? He's somewhat deaf, you know; he lost the hearing of one ear in the service. He could have an operation for nothing. But he never will.

"Who needs another hole in the head? One's enough."

It was April; the wind was blowing fresh tender soot, swirling papers fancifully in the gutters of Uptown—my grand-mother's neighborhood. The sky was heavy and full of gloom, but here and there, a splinter, a gleam. Rudy pulled into the thick of the grimy, sluggish traffic—deaf or indifferent to our female conversation.

I couldn't believe we were going to talk about Roxanne's hair all the way to the wedding.

Roxanne is Uncle Rudy's young wife, a big handsome

Southern girl, raw-boned, rock-jawed, her pale head dropped over her knitting. Peculiarly pale; translucent, like rock candy, and almost as brittle. It was stiff with spray lacquer.

"Oh, you did something to your hair," my mother remarked as we climbed in back.

"I don't like it," Roxanne said at once, without glancing round or lifting her head. Her bare shoulders were scarcely moving in their sockets as she yanked at her yarn and plucked at her needles. "I tolt her beige blont and she dit it silver blont instet." She spoke in her discontented mountain drawl.

"Go back and make them do it over," my mother said. "You pay enough, don't you?" Talk about needles.

"It smells pretty, though," my grandmother said, sniffing through the glitter of rhinestone frames.

Roxanne flicked the yarn irritably over her forefinger. "I don't like it."

And so on.

But sometimes it seems that's all these occasions are really for. "Aren't you going to put on any makeup?" my mother asked as soon as I walked in the door. "Look how thin she's getting," my grandmother said, catching her lip between her teeth. "She's putting on weight," said my mother.

Even my grandmother is all dolled up. A little old lady, shrunken with age, gazing from between shoulders hunched with arthritis. Swollen crippled fingers clasping her coat, the lapels weighted down with dime-store brooches. She loves adornment. There was a pause just before, as we were leaving her flat; she wanted to retrieve her watch—a big Timex with a Spandex band, a man's watch. The utilitarian chunk of nickel plating dangled from her fingertips. Her stiff fingers stretching the band, dragging it over her wrist. She's eighty-three and she's even more obstinate. Her children beg her to come and live with them, get out of that wretched neighborhood. Now their own children are marrying, they all have room—they'd love to have her. But she knows better. At her age, it's bad enough being mortal, without having to make apologies for it too.

"Hey? Which way you going?"

My mother sat up, suddenly erect, her striking white head looking all about. She was in black and white from head to toe, stark contrasts: dark mink stole, long evening skirt, pointed shoes. "I thought you were going to take Sheridan."

"Hah. We'd be there tomorrow, I took Sheridan," Rudy said, looking over his shoulder and showing the dark spaces in his teeth. He has a loud offended voice, the result of his partial deafness.

"You don't mean to tell me you're taking the Edens Expressway?"

"Nacherly. What do you think? I'm taking Edens."

"Edens. Who ever heard of anything so stupid? Taking Edens."

My mother was rummaging in her purse. She took out a mimeographed sheet—a map of directions to the church, in one of the northernmost suburbs; it had come with the invitations—and shoved it across the seat at her brother's big back.

"Here. Look. You go straight out Sheridan, you'll be there in fifteen minutes."

"You should of driven your own car, you wanted to take Sheridan." Rudy sat unmoved, eyes level, watching traffic in the mirror.

"I woultn't say nothing more if I was you." Roxanne turned sideways in her seat to view my mother. "We're liable to ent up in Milwaukee. You know how stubborn Rooty is."

Yes, and he's had riot training.

But my mother does not know how to desist. The irresistible force meets the immovable object. A routine encounter for her.

After a while she sat back, however, and began whispering

to me, stating her case, thrusting the map under my nose. I had already been en route an hour and a half, just to get to my grandmother's house, and I couldn't make heads or tails of it. That displeased her. She got angrier with me, rattling the piece of paper in my face. Her own face startlingly sallow under her beautiful white hair. She must have seen I had no sympathy with her, either. I couldn't help that; my mother's panic is an old and potent enemy of mine.

It was now noon; the wedding was called for twelve-thirty. "And when they say twelve-thirty they mean *twelve-thirty,"* my mother said, laying her hand to her cheek. "That's not Jewish time, you know."

As a patrolman on the city payroll, Rudy has to live in Chicago. My parents do too. My father hates grass; golf courses and cemeteries give him the creeps. But one of the reasons my grandmother would never consider moving in with her other children is that she finds life in the suburbs so dull. She likes to be able to see lots of people, to sit in a lobby somewhere and watch the world go by. All she asks is a lobby.

In her neighborhood, with all the grim apartment hotels for the elderly, the shelter homes and halfway houses, there are plenty of lobbies. The one in her building is no good, however —too dark, off to one side, you miss everything—so she prefers to sit in the large plate-glass window of the A & P, resting her shopping bags. You see lots of old ladies sitting there.

Her next-door neighbor is confined to her room and keeps the door open, buoyed up among her pillows like a pile of life preservers. She has a darkened, pewtery complexion; you feel the gleam of eyes on you. Though she's hearty enough— banging her cane against the wall to get your attention.

Today, when I had alighted from the elevator, both doors were open; my grandmother was going back and forth between the two rooms, keeping her neighbor company. She introduced us. "My granddaughter! My son! My daughter!" She was proud of her visitors, because we were dressed up for the wedding.

My mother, as it happens, was still getting dressed—presenting her back, all unzippered, to the wide-open doorway, her long skirts hiked up about her hips, fastening her garters.

"So what do you call this, Mother?" I said.

"Hmmm," she replied airily, as she bent over her black stockings. "Nobody ever comes by here anyway."

And yet she is the first to complain about the suspicious types lurking in the elevators and passageways. They need encouragement. This is what you call flinging down the gauntlet. My mother was also taking the opportunity to announce that her charms were all used up. ("Who's going to bother with an old woman?") Not so, by the way.

Compared to other buildings in Uptown, this one is not all that bad: a tall, yellow-brick "elevator building," its roof rising high above the squat burned-out three-flats and boarded storefronts of Sheridan Road. The entrance, stripped bare, has the naked gleam of a ballroom; the dim narrow pier-glass mirrors hark back to its days of luxury.

As we were passing through today, my grandmother was suddenly reminded: last week, one of the tenants—a large old man, broad-shouldered, one eye dim behind a smoked lens: I knew which one—got robbed on the bus. He had just cashed a pension check, eighty dollars. He sat in his shirtsleeves in the lobby, telling the others all about it. There wasn't much to tell. He had the money in his pockets when he got on the bus, it wasn't there when he got off. His fingers felt about his chest, still groping in his pockets for the money, as if it might turn up yet.

All at once he stiffened in his chair; his heart jumped beneath his shirtfront. He stretched himself out dead.

"So it turned out that *jener* [the other; she meant the pickpocket] needed that money worse than he did," she said. That's what I like about the old lady; she's so sentimental.

By the time we got to the church, the ceremony had already started, the backs of heads gazing toward the altar. The church itself seemed rattlingly empty; row upon row of varnished pews, and only the white sheet down the middle aisle to indicate the trappings of a wedding. I'd heard it would be small and simple, but there was something intimidating about such austerity. I crept into the last pew on the aisle in back, my mother and her mother following arm in arm. The old lady —well under five feet—shuffled along with her head thrust forward, looking both wary and determined. A few other latecomers hurried in, crossed themselves with a sprinkle of holy water, and—stooping quickly on the aisle—slid onto the bench at the other end.

It was the first I had realized that Millicent was Catholic, though I knew that her parents had objected to her marrying my cousin Gregg. (As they had objected when Gregory and Millicent traveled through Europe together. "If it was *my* daughter, I wouldn't let her go," Uncle Leon had reassured them.) I don't know what Gregory considers himself.

Long-legged in his striped pants and frock coat, he was standing with his hands clasped in front of him, swaying lightly. I could just glimpse the edges of his swarthy mustache. Millicent looked very tall in her white veil, with her long black hair curling down her back beneath the train.

Rudy came strolling in with his hands in his pockets, the vents of his jacket split over his hips. It was broad daylight in the lofty empty church: brighter than daylight, light spilling solemnly from the high arched windows. He looked like a monolith, wading through the pews. Glancing back and scowling at us over his shoulder—wondering what we were doing, of course, sitting all the way in back and on the wrong side; the bride's side.

The priest asked us to rise.

At once my eye was attracted to Uncle Leon's handsome white head—the same arresting white mane as my mother's. From the back, his figure seemed as youthful, as broad-shouldered and narrow-waisted in his frockcoat, as Gregory's; and he was standing in the same way—his hands clasped in front of him, swaying forward on his toes; light on his feet. I don't know why I had never noticed the resemblance before. Women are always telling Leon how handsome he is: dark Latin features, bushy black brows.

"Ah, I wish they wouldn't," Aunt Irene will say, laughing good-naturedly. "There's no living with him after."

A robust, pleasing matron herself; brown-haired, red-cheeked, beaming, a bosom like a tea service; a Quaker from the Lebanon Valley. She met Leon at Valley Forge; he a wounded corporal, she a hospital administrator. For him she joined the Wacs. In those days she could shake down her stoical braids and sit on her hair, all ripples and waves. Everyone knows that Leon raised the general level of intelligence, energy, capability, industry in our family several notches when he brought Irene into it. Yet after twenty-five years she is still the outsider. She's not Jewish. And everyone is sure that Irene, for her part, is still anti-Semitic. And why not? If our own prejudices are any indication.

Some crevices run deep. It used to be that at election time my uncle and his wife would make a pact: they promised each other that neither of them would vote, since their votes would only cancel out. Irene is a Republican, straight down the line; Leon is a party Democrat, one X in the box and that's it. But each would sneak off to vote just the same, so now they ignore politics.

Again the priest asked us to rise. By this time my mother had begun to whisper, leaning down in her dark fur. My grandmother couldn't negotiate these ups and downs and was staring ahead, biting her lip with concentration.

"Do you think she's *Catholic?*" my mother was saying. "No one told us she was *Catholic.*"

Bride and groom turned around to accept the offertory. The bride's dark-browed face, broad in its headdress, suddenly, unexpectedly, shone upon us. It was burning, fiercely beautiful. *The Lord bless you and keep you and make His face to shine upon you. . . .* For the first time all day I remembered what it was all about, felt privileged to be a witness. And everyone must have felt it. People came to their senses. There was almost a sigh of relief. The altar boy in his full black skirts crouched, quivering the brass bells; smoke fumed from the censers. Millicent lifted her veil to take communion. Gregory did not take it.

"*Jewish?*" the ladies on the other side of me were whispering among themselves. "You really think he's a *Jew?*"

I had waited fifteen minutes for a bus and when it came it wasn't an express. The expresses weren't running. The express goes from Hyde Park directly onto the Outer Drive, and it takes twenty minutes to get downtown. The local takes forty, fifty minutes. And it meanders through the South Side slums. At this point I could have walked a block or so to the Illinois Central commuter station, and caught a train as far as the Loop. But it was going to be a day when my inertia was great. I got on the bus and sat down by a window in back and opened a book on my lap.

I always take books with me on buses or trains. I never read them. Years ago when I was an undergraduate at the university, I used to travel three hours a day on these same buses, commuting between the South Side campus and my home on the West Side. "You can get all your studying done," that's what people would say. But I never got any studying done; I'd sit with the whole pile of books on my lap (I remember the thick green volumes of *The People Shall Judge*), looking out the window. Three hours a day, an hour and a half each way, staring at the same sights out the same windows. I was fifteen then; it's possible that all this travel was stupefying me. Still, it seems to me that there is something immoral—because inattentive—about reading when your body is in transit. And maybe I felt even then that I should be paying attention instead. But paying attention to what?

I glanced up the aisle. The thing I'd forgotten was how the bus kept turning. Up Fifty-first Street to Drexel; down Drexel to Forty-seventh; up Forty-seventh to Martin Luther King Drive; down King to Forty-third . . . Every few blocks it nosed onward, plunging deeper and deeper into the black ghetto. The coins clicked and rolled in the fare box.

The South Side has always been Chicago's black belt; these slums were here years before I was born. But in the past, when I used to travel back and forth this way almost every day, I never noticed if I was white and all the other passengers were black. Blacks had not yet pressed the issue. And it must be said right off that the fact that I didn't notice, that it didn't matter to me, did not improve the situation in any way.

I remember becoming fully aware of this discrepancy reading *Native Son,* when the rich girl and her Communist boyfriend think that their liberal sentiments will make up to Bigger for everything. The trouble is that these one-to-one solutions—I love you, you love me; you shoot me, I shoot you —are no good. Just no use. Still, this ignorance or innocence or whatever you want to call it was long gone—and I would have given a great deal to have it back again. Today I was very much aware of the color of everyone else's skin, and I was sure that everyone on the bus was just as much aware of mine.

This was manifestly not so. No one was paying attention to me, any more than I was paying attention to the pages of the book lying open on my lap. As a matter of fact, almost everyone else seemed to be reading—the news sheets crackling, the murder black in the headlines.

The bus was getting crowded; passengers swayed in the aisle and grappled for the strap hangers. A girl was groping her way, arm over arm, along the rails, an unlighted cigarette in her fingers. Hot pants, vinyl stretch boots, turban. Her face flat, expressionless, artificially pale—an Oriental effect. She leaned her shaved eyebrows over my seat.

"Gotta match?"

I gave her matches.

This has got to stop. I've got to stop reacting to people according to color. This is what has been happening to me; happening to everyone I know. White and black. Race is a prominent fact of life in Chicago, a partitioned city, walled and wired. You can't help reacting in this way. Try it. Try it walking down the street some night. It's a reflex. Everyone is becoming conditioned. And for some reason I realized this all of a sudden listening to the news this morning, realized that I've been allowing myself to become conditioned—letting this fear, this racism, run away with me. I'm not sure why a murder in the streets—even around the corner—should have had such a bracing effect. But you've got to come up for air sometime; maybe that's why I got on the bus today. I used to know these things.

The sign on the parking lot gate said: "Left Turn Only," so Rudy turned right. The rest of the cars had already gone off, leaving the church in a motorcade for the motel where the wedding reception would be held. But not us. Roxy was studying the map.

"It's right around the corner."

12

As a matter of fact, we were at Fort Sheridan, the army base. I used to think it was much farther when I was a little girl and Rudy was stationed there. Now the low-lying motels all around were not that easy to distinguish from the barracks, the tracks of wire fences.

"Hey. How come you guys sat on the wrong side of the church?" Rudy asked. "The bride's side, dummies. How come you didn't come up front with the rest of the family? What's the matter with you? Don't you like to see what's going on?"

"All that standing and kneeling," my mother said. "I'm exhausted. Nuts to that. I didn't know it was going to be a *Catholic* ceremony."

"I coult've tolt you right away if I lookt at the invitation," Roxy said. "Only I never even lookt at the invitation." She's Immersion Baptist, I think.

I was wondering about this business of bride's side, groom's side. Partitions and more partitions. Why do we always have to take sides? How primitive are these divisions?

Roxy jerked a thumb at the window. "You turn right at this corner. Right at the stop sign."

Rudy went straight.

"Hey, you big jerk. You shoult've turnt back there." Roxy looked round, still jerking her thumb. "He't get lost for sure if I din't tell him."

"I think he must be doing it on purpose," I said.

"You don't say," my mother said, the corner of her mouth grim against her cheek.

In a minute the road disappeared, we came to a leafy dead end, a bower of branches, and Rudy had to back the car out through the trees.

By the time we got to the motel, the reception line had broken formation; the bride and groom were off having their pictures taken, and guests were milling around the pleasant blue room with its huge fireplace and shimmer of chandeliers. Gas flames licked and curled about the artificial logs; champagne glasses were being filled as quickly as they were snatched from the trays. When I have the chance, I always drink champagne.

I wasn't at the shower, so I hadn't met any of Millicent's family before. Her father was a slight dark man with a stiff highball splashing and jostling in his fist. Sober, a plumber with four daughters to marry off, footing the bill for all these bashes. His wife was elegant, blond, slender; and the four strapping girls, of course, are all bouncingly beautiful. So it looks as if Gregg, like his father, has done all right for himself. This was the gist of the intelligence report I had already received from my mother.

"You know me, one drink and I'm out," she said, tripping up in her long skirts and holding her glass aloft to show it was empty. It's true; usually she gets dazzling and giddy. But today she didn't seem at all light-headed to me; and everywhere I looked I kept seeing her—my mother has a way of standing out in a crowd—her black-and-white dress grimly prominent, like the priests in their habits.

"Someone asked me who I was and I forgot my name," Aunt Sylvia said. My mother's younger sister: a helmet of smooth iron hair, earrings swinging at her cheeks. She had been on the Weight Watchers diet and her pretty face was thin, looked pinched, a little sour (the intelligence report from my grandmother)—and she was smoking; she never used to. Holding the cigarette at arm's length, tapping the ashes over the gold tips of her shoes.

"Guess what. Gary called up from school and told us to break out the champagne." Gary is her son.

"He's getting married?" my mother asked.

"No. He got a job."

The job was at Zenith Radio, where Sylvia herself used to work during the war years when my Uncle Fred was in service. They married on furlough. I remember very well—she lived with us at the time—her going off to work in her baggy-seated overalls, her hair bound in a turban with the black curls springing out on top. She was on the assembly line. Gary will have an executive position: fourteen thousand to start. A lot more than Fred makes as a printer.

My grandmother was sitting at an empty table, surveying the field of preparations, the white cloths, the busboys filling sparkling water glasses. She was waiting to be called by the photographer. She always says she hates to have her picture taken, but I noticed her slipping off her glasses and dropping them into her purse. Without the funny rhinestone frames, the iridescent lenses, she looks suddenly—bushy brows, coarse powerful white hair and slanted cheeks—like a shaman. Her dress of some green wizard material, the shimmering jacket bunched under her heavy brooches.

As a younger woman my grandmother never used to have this personal vanity, she never cared for such things. But now her copyright has expired, so to speak; she has entered the public domain. She clutched her purse to her lap, smoothing back her strong hair with stiff misshapen fingers.

And now Millicent's grandmother was brought up for an introduction: two old matriarchs. A large woman listing heavily on a cane; vigorous, in her corsets, with the silver rinse in her hair. She's in her eighties too, her complexion darkened with age spots, tarnished almost—like the neighbor with her pillow cushions. She had been opposed all along to the marriage because Gregg—or at least his father—is Jewish. The last holdout in the family; the wedding had been delayed to appease her.

"You must come and take tea with me sometime," she said,

grasping my grandmother's hand. And then, hesitating—wondering about our rituals—"Or *coffee,*" she added, shaking emphatically.

"When are *you* going to get married?" Uncle Rudy asked, towering over me. His hands were in his pockets and his gaze strayed automatically over the small milling groups—a head above the crowd—checking them out.

"I've already been; I don't have to," I said.

"So you wouldn't get married a second time?"

"Would you?" I said, sipping from the rim of the thin-stemmed glass.

He shrugged; his elbows flapped against his sides. "Huh. I didn't want to get married the first time," he said in his dull monotone, still peering all about. He looked like a hawk. That's the trouble with Rudy; you can never tell. You can't tell when he's putting it on, just pretending to be thick, slow, deaf, stubborn. Everyone knows he can't be as dumb as he makes out.

Now he seemed to have something on his mind. "How come nobody tells them?" he said. We were both looking toward Sylvia's daughter, Mindy—almost gravely pretty with her long thin exposed legs, long heavy hair. Hers will be the next wedding. Rudy took my arm, urging.

"Go ahead. Say something. Tell her."

"I know, but you can't," I said. "It's not fair."

"Oh. Uh huh." And his head bobbed up and down. "It's not fair."

Uncle Fred had gathered a crowd. Telling dirty jokes again? Sylvia was fretting because they were to be seated at the same table as the Fathers. "I just hope he behaves himself." But this was serious. He was surrounded by Millicent's mother and aunts and scarcely glanced our way as we came up, going on in his tight-lipped, hissing whisper. It was Gary's job again—evidently this subject was of the most intense interest. I didn't understand the significance of this at first. The wedding itself was a sort of truce: it was the subject of Gary's job that really seemed to be uniting everybody.

Sylvia worked as a clerk to put Gary and Mindy through school; Irene has been waiting on tables for years. These blond aunts of Millicent's, with their freckled cheeks, must have done the same. Now the job market had collapsed; a college degree was almost a liability. Millicent is substitute teaching. Gregg was teaching driving, but has turned up something better—still temporary—with the Welfare. Mindy has been looking for almost a year for a teaching position; her fiancé will be graduating this summer with another useless certificate. Wherever you turned, the story was the same. But now that the situation is so bad—so reminiscent—it isn't the kids who are worrying either: they are going to school, marrying, traveling to Europe all the same. It's the parents—the plumbers, the printers—the same class who have borne the brunt of things all along, who are still worrying about the future.

I noticed the contact lens over Fred's eye. An old shrapnel wound, quiescent for twenty-five years; all of a sudden it's starting to act up again. It gives his expression a peculiar urgency. All my uncles are damaged with war wounds. There's Rudy's deafness, his loud injured voice. And Leon—strutting among the white tables in his pleated shirt front—is lame in one arm. Striking a match with his thumb, he lets it hang by his side. A funny thing about Leon. He's a scofflaw. He'll go out of his way to park illegally. He'll drive around the block looking for a No Parking sign or a nice little fire hydrant.

What was secretly depressing everyone was this: After seven years of a sacrificially expensive university education, Gary will be earning about the same money as Rudy—a city of Chicago patrolman, a "pig," who had to be trundled through high school in a wheelbarrow. Rudy makes a better living than any man in the family, and Rudy is the one who is supposed to be so stupid. It rankles. And—to top it all off, and as if to rub it in—he has nothing to show for it. A dilapidated apartment, a car that isn't paid for; the little boy is cross-eyed and they're saving up for an operation, there isn't a penny in the bank. (It seems that everybody knows their business.) And he and his wife don't get along either; there is rancor to go with all the squalor. No one can understand such a life. They feel sorry for, irritated with Rudy. Rudy and Roxanne seldom show up at these family occasions.

"Who's taking care of the children?" Sylvia asked, looking up at Roxy. Roxanne is six-foot-one in her stocking feet, statuesque, immobile, like a Las Vegas showgirl. But she complains she has no pep, and goes to her doctor to get liver shots. My mother had already asked her that question; everybody kept asking her. It's an unwritten law: as soon as a harassed mother gets out of the house for a couple of hours, everyone has to ask her who's taking care of the children.

"They're olt enough to take care of themselves," she said tartly.

I still have custody, but since my two sons are older they have gone to live with their father, and now I'm the one who gets to see them only on school vacations. They had just gone back a few days before, and I missed them. It's not such a bad arrangement; I'm not complaining. In some ways it's too good, too rich—we are just skimming the cream. Only I believe that life—a real life—is lived day to day.

There is this to be said for it, however: at least no one asks me who's taking care of the children. Indeed, no one ever asks me much. I'm not married; my ID isn't validated, so to speak. Weddings are the worst; they don't know where to put me, what to do with me. Today I'm not even getting grilled about the usual topics—the crime and the "colored." I was glad to see the dishes being wheeled in, gleaming tiers on the service carts.

The best man—even swarthier than Gregg, with a more pendulous mustache—was offering his arm to my grandmother. Still time for one last picture: she was much in demand. She leaned on his dark sleeve. She won't use a cane.

"Oh, how little she's getting," Sylvia remarked, biting her lip as she looked after the old lady. A habit she gets from her mother. "She used to be as tall as I am."

The thing is, I don't feel sorry for my grandmother. I don't think it's a shame that she's so old. I love her with admiration, not out of pity. She's probably the only member of my family who doesn't wrench it out of me that way.

At table, over fresh fruit cup and sherbet—the old lady with her back to the licking logs of the fireplace, her green jacket glowing in the flames—everyone started complaining about my father. He was in Israel, visiting my sister and the other set of grandchildren, and the postcards he was sending back were all identical.

"That's nothing," my mother said. It seemed she had just received two letters from him, and they were also exactly alike. "He just doesn't know how to write a letter, poor man."

Letters. Who expects letters? I'm supposed to be tickled he talks to me. But this is true, if I may judge from the five or six letters I have received from him in my life. Stilted, formal, almost to the point of illiteracy—all the more because he writes a scribe's hand, slanting and fluid. Palmer method; he won prizes for his handwriting in grammar school. And it's as if someone had written them down for him, at his embarrassed dictation:

Be a Good Girl. Apply Yourself. Obey Your Mother. Dont Disappoint . . . Your Dad.

My mother was working in a summer camp then; my sister and I used to spend our whole summer away from home, and

I would miss my father bitterly. Crouching homesick in my lower bunk—with its coarse army surplus blanket, the damp smell of rotting wood—reading these spartan lines over and over, his moralizing tone bewildered and bereaved me. What had I done wrong? What was I going to do? How did he know about it? But that seemed to be his prerogative; my father is a natural moralist. Almost as big as my Uncle Rudy and far more powerful; he can fix anything, though his hands look thick and clumsy, capable only of brute strength. Once he lifted the back of a truck when a fellow worker was trapped under it. What I like about this story is its sequel, so typical of my father's fortunes, his outlook, his whole life. The man he had saved never spoke to him again, shunned his company, couldn't look him in the eye.

Last summer my father fell off a ladder while fixing the roof of a house (he's one of these obsolete men who maintain things). His size and strength added to the dread I felt in the hospital, observing his helplessness: a big broken creature, gray-fleshed—the slick wet-mop grayness of internal bleeding —being lifted and turned by little Filipino nurses. How they accomplished this was a mystery, for they would pull the canvas curtains about his bed before they assayed such a task. When I heard the noises behind the drawn curtains, watched the blips on the heart monitor while he lay laboriously breathing—his heart was leaking—I felt something like the pangs I used to feel when I read his letters in summer camp. There was a persistency of tone. Reproach. I was wondering, if he left like this, how I would live with it.

His trip to the Holy Land was a Pilgrimage after his Reprieve (his words, naturally). Passing silver sauce boats, baskets of crusty rolls, spearing icy butter pats (I always have trouble), I started thinking what it would be like to get a letter from my father. What if I tore open the airmail envelope—

blue as distances—and confronted once again the same old phrases in the same sloping hand:

Be a Good Girl. Tend to Business. Try to Make the Best of It. Don't Disappoint . . . Your Dad.

The meal was excellent. Waitresses hovered, the photographer stalked, screwing the lens to his eye. He'd fling up one arm and stiffen suddenly, lifeless, dangling from it.

"Take off your glasses," my mother cautioned, knocking my arm with her elbow as he flashed our picture.

She was dissatisfied with me, and that's how it comes out. How well I know. Every time I have seen my mother for the last twenty years, she has made a remark about my hair. It's getting discouraging, to know this beforehand. People could get the idea we have nothing to say. And yet I found myself reacting to her in the same way—noticing all through the meal that she seemed to talk only when her mouth was full and her cheek was bulging like a fist. As if she were chewing a quid of tobacco, and about to squirt. Alarming. Her sallow cheek. She was having a bad day. Bitter, discolored, dry-eyed. I still wish I had been kinder.

The groom rose to make a toast. Slouched in his tux, rocking on his heels, like his father; a dark symmetrical mustache. "I guess there's everyone in this room who means anything to me," he began, lifting his glass. Everyone was touched; it was as if we had had to be reminded all over again: applause, murmurs, rose gratefully from the white circles of the tables. There was a clatter of dishes being carted away.

My grandmother, of course, doesn't eat meat out; it's not kosher. And we had forgotten to order her fish. The waitress looked at her plate. "You finished?" eying the damp red slice of meat.

The old lady turned herself stiffly sideways to peer at the

sound, since she can't move her neck. Her voice rang out. "Take it away."

She hadn't touched her food. She hadn't carried on, hadn't complained, though it was all in the script. She was watching them cutting up the wedding cake, rapidly distributing slices over the scraps and crumbs of the tables.

"Wrap up a slice for me," she commanded my mother, pointing her big distorted finger. "I want to bring home for the *goy.*" (She meant her neighbor.)

My children's father descends in a direct line from a Pilgrim who fell overboard during the voyage of the *Mayflower.* "A lustie younge man," Governor Bradford describes him, who held long and fast to the halyards, "sundrie fadomes under water," until they hauled him in out of the lurching sea. Since then the family had considerably loosened its grip. Papa was a medievalist, a Prof at Indiana U., and they lived way out in a grand Victorian relic. I thought it was grand. There were raccoons in the attic—the shell-like claws left perfect tracks in the powder the exterminator had sprinkled; and in the bathroom—an afterthought, a cul-de-sac squeezed under the stairs, all eaves and crannies—you got the most delicious sense of privacy, as if all the world might forget that it and you were there. A grim reminder, however, was the mark painted about two inches up from the curved bottom of the bathtub, indicating the permissible water level. The same thing they did in the bathtubs of Buckingham Palace during the war.

The fact is, my in-laws were *tight.* Not the scraping, face-saving, working-class thrift I was used to; they were flagrantly, *shamelessly* stingy. The virtue of the faded WASP aristocracy. Papa would cook up a stew of beef and carrots at the beginning of the week, and start adding oatmeal and water toward the end. And he would follow you about, animated, talking (he was still greatly exercised over the persecution of the

Albigensians), systematically switching off all the electric lights. This was a hazard, no joke, since the house was crammed to the rafters. He had to climb up a stepladder to fetch down his books; there was furniture on top of the furniture; my mother-in-law, still a porcelain beauty, without a chip or a crack, collected antiques. He kept magazines, newspapers, yellowed files, in her cradle rockers and canopied cribs and native hammocks and even in the upright commode stools. And yet they were "only camping," she told me—in this house whose every niche and shingle they had penetrated, occupied, swelling and expanding like the rock-wool insulation they had had pumped in, blown through a giant snorkel. Even at that time they had lived in Indiana over thirty years. But what's thirty years to a New England blueblood? They were ready to move back "at the drop of a hat."

Now there were only two sons left, the last of the line, and one a confirmed bachelor. This branch had lost most of their money about nineteen-ought-five—before any of my progenitors had so much as stepped off the boat. What the family needed was some fresh stock, "hybrid vigor." They were "sick of their washed-out New England blood." Thus Papa, thrilled at the prospect of having a Jewish daughter-in-law, breeding with the race—for he believed that all Jews were cultured, cosmopolitan, intellectual, and rich. I had never run into this wacky Puritan Jew-worship before, for obvious reasons: I didn't fit the description, and I didn't know anybody who did.

What the dear old man thought when he took a half day off from his duties at the university (only time he *would* take; he had seven years' leave accumulated and untouched at his retirement, which had been forestalled through a special act of the state legislature), what he thought when he took his half day off in honor of the wedding and came up for the afternoon on the *James Whitcomb Riley,* what he thought when he finally met me and my family, I don't rightly know. I wasn't getting any bargain either. And it doesn't matter, because he was right about the "hybrids."

"Now listen, you guys," I said, as the automobiles were pulling up to the carpeted canopy. "I'd like to get home sometime today, so please don't go nagging Rudy any more. Leave him alone. He's the driver—let him do what he wants."

"All right, all right," said my mother.

"She promist, I din't," said Roxanne, poking round in her bag for her knitting.

It had turned out to be a nice day after all; the sun had finally come out in the late afternoon, resting on luminous banks of clouds. The sky was blue as chalk. Rudy drove with exaggerated tenderness—like the Sunday driver he was pretending to be—taking Sheridan Road, the scenic route home, to please my mother. The road wound and dipped through wooded ravines, still rusty brown with winter's oak leaves. Here and there a glimpse of a cantilevered terrace, a glassed-in porch, a cathedral ceiling. We used to drive out this way sometimes on Sundays when I was a child, to ooh and aah at these sights, the half-hidden homes of the rich. These are the affluent North Shore suburbs.

A little red convertible, a Fiat Spider with the top down, cut in front of us. The driver had very short, shaggy, windblown yellow hair and the roots were dark as the center of a daisy.

"There!" Roxanne said, growing somewhat animated, for her, and pointing the bright tip of her knitting needle. "That's the color my hair was suppost to be."

The little car sped off in a burst of exhaust and lost us quickly on the winding road. Roxanne sank back, curving her spine and clicking her needles.

"Well, I'm just glad Pa [their father] wasn't there to see *that,*" said my mother at last. "It would make him feel *terrible.*" She shrugged her mink stole round her shoulders. "It just doesn't work out. It's much better when two people have the same background. It makes for a better chance in a marriage."

"Is that how come you get along so good with your own husband?" Rudy said, eying her in the mirror. "You got the same background?"

"I wasn't speaking *personally,*" she said.

My mother always says what she is thinking; only what could she be thinking *of?* Rudy and Roxanne in the front seat, bigger than life; her own daughter sitting right beside her. And if you observe that my marriage was a failure, and that Rudy and Roxanne are no great success, that doesn't make her remarks seem more tactful. But it was a little late in the day for tact—it was sink or swim, every man for himself. And what bothered me was where she was at, what sort of world she must be living in. The fact is, with the exception of my sister (and *that's* a holy mess I won't go into), no one in my mother's family has married a Jew in the last thirty years. Which means that by now half her own relatives are not Jews. But never mind; she still sees her family as average, normal, the salt of the earth. Jewish.

Of course, I know where she was at. She was reliving the scene of her own greatest humiliation—the day of my wedding. Only now, each time this scene is repeated, she finds herself older, less resilient, stonier—more isolated. A ship in drydock. She adjusted her furs, offended, while we stopped for a train-crossing. Bells shrilling, lights flashing and winking back and forth. The heavy boxcars knocked and shuddered over the tracks; the hood of the car glimmered. We were staring straight into the flat red disk of the setting sun.

It dawned on me. We were supposed to be heading south and east—not west. And there are no train-crossings on Sheridan Road.

We were elsewhere.

"Oh, for God's sake, Uncle Rudy," I said, shouting over the

noise. "What is this? Don't you know I have to get back to the South Side yet."

Roxanne's face lighted up. "You're the one that sait it, I din't," she said, turning round with a granite grin at the back seat.

After the student murder a few months ago, there were stirrings in the Hyde Park community. First-aid courses, an emergency switchboard service. It had taken almost an hour to get the victim to the hospital, with his fourteen stab wounds, and he bled to death. The purpose of first aid, switchboards, is to keep people from bleeding to death in the streets. And it makes all the rest of us, bystanders, supernumeraries, feel more effective. But these are after all only *ex-post facto,* one-to-one solutions. It all reminds me, weirdly, of the fallout-shelter craze of the early sixties, when people were digging holes in back yards, sinking concrete blocks, stocking up with canned goods, flashlight batteries, shovels, rifles. The point is, these people were preparing for nuclear attack; they were accepting it as an eventuality—they were acquiescing. One questioned the quality of such survivors.

This was called civil defense. And telephones and tourniquets are obviously civil defense measures too; the similarity is no accident. The latest thing is a campaign to distribute whistles; you're supposed to keep them handy, wear them around your neck, blow them—after an attack.

None of this is going to stop the conditioning.

Now that nights are warmer—windows open to the darkness, artillery noises from the streets—you sense it all the more. The fear is quicker. Besides, everyone knows that violence increases with fair weather. Numbers only assert, but at least a dozen women I know have been raped, beaten and terrorized. The nature of the crime is significant: we are a passive population under siege. This anarchy, the flashing of guns and knives, may as well be martial law; there may as well be curfew in the deserted streets.

You feel stranded after dark. The air is penetrating. Particularly in Hyde Park, with the ghosts of the old stockyards to the west, and to the south—very much alive, a red glow from my windows—the inner sanctums of the steel mills. Like the days after King's assassination—the odor of smoke and cinders blowing over the city. The slums were burning. The conditions I describe are only a dim reflection of the terror of that life.

"He wasn't a member of a gang or anything," a black mother is quoted in the papers after the slaughter of her son. "Someone at Ribs-'n'-Bibs just thought David was laughing at him."

In the meantime all this is a topic of dinner-table conversation. Our fear is becoming socialized. Moving is a constant theme. One friend who has been raped, burglarized, and had her car stolen (three separate occasions), is still considering leaving Hyde Park. Plenty of reasons for leaving. The rents are as high here as almost anywhere in the city, and the food prices are even higher—typical of slum communities, a captive market. No competition. There is only one movie house in all Hyde Park; indeed, for many miles around. Restaurants and businesses close early. More and more they close for good. There are no gathering places, no lively night life. How could there be? People are afraid to go out after dark. It is just an island surrounded by the defoliation of the slums.

And yet none of these are real motivations for leaving. The fact is that most people have come to Hyde Park in the first place just because of the things it did not have. (It doesn't have relatives, for instance.) And I realized this morning that "security" is not the main thing either. "Security" is an expensive illusion. We can't all climb into the fallout shelters. In my grandmother's neighborhood, Uptown, it's the notorious desolation, the poverty, that is the constant reminder of what the real facts are; in my neighborhood—so much more green and affluent from its rooftops—it is the tension between black and white. And I suspect that the real reason people want to leave is not so much that they think they will be "safer" anywhere else; or so that they will be able to go out to a movie: it is because they don't like their own automatic responses any more. That's what they want to get away from. They want to halt the conditioning that is dehumanizing us.

"Aren't you going to come in?" Rudy asked, sticking his big head in at the window. We weren't planning to, had only stopped long enough to drop Roxy off so she could get back to the children. But Rudy seemed disappointed.

"Her," he said, lifting his chin at me. "I want her to come in and see my wallpaper."

With anyone else this might have meant that he had something he wanted to say to me in private. But not with Rudy. That will never happen; Rudy will never speak his heart. I followed his ponderous shoulders into the house.

The landlord lives upstairs, and his side of the front porch is even more sagging, swaying and peeling than theirs. But the rent is cheap, and they have a sort of mutual nonaggression pact: they won't expect any repairs, he won't expect any raises. He's an old Swede, gaunt, bald, toothless, deaf, and he just doesn't want to be bothered. Something Rudy understands.

Rudy is an honest cop. When my high school sweetheart joined the force—"I wish I thought of it years ago; I'd a owned three apartment buildings by now"—Rudy told me right away he'd never last. "They don't want that kind no more." I'm sorry I don't know who turned out to be right; but the point is, Rudy is not a cynic. And anybody has enough brains to be cynical. He is immutable, incorruptible; that is the real truth of his nature. How could you buy him? How could you approach him? He has no greed, he has no vanity, no ambition. A threat would only provoke his obstinacy—the most powerful force of all. It would be like trying to bribe Starved Rock.

As soon as we got inside, Rudy pointed to the wallpaper in the living room, a crowded flocked pattern on a gold ground. "Roxy put it up." He stroked the wall.

"When was that?"

"It's been two years," Roxy said.

Rudy pulled my sleeve. "Come see the wallpaper in the kitchen." The vinyl pattern covered the ceiling. "Roxy put it up with a broom," Rudy told me, gazing up at the high ceiling from his gloomy height. Unmade beds, unwashed cups, cigarette butts, dishes in the sink; it's like a frat house. But Roxy is very handy, and she knits, crochets, sews to perfection—the handicrafts of her Kentucky hills. It makes the stuff you see for sale in expensive boutiques look disgraceful, I'm not kidding. Call that a quilt? Shame on them. They should see Roxy's patchwork, Roxy's coverlets, her shawls, stuffed animals. Her skill is the result of a long tradition, of which she is the end. Rudy showed off her projects. "Roxy did this too?"

The children in the meantime had gone out to the car to say hello. In a minute the little boy in his long pants and baseball jacket—his big glasses wider than his face—came dashing in, bursting with excitement. "Guess who's in the car?" he said, grinning up at us through thick dark frames, balancing their weight. One eye tugged at its inner corner. *"Bobbe! Bobbe!"*

He took off again. His shoes knocked with a heavy tread.

I was fetching a glass of water for my grandmother. Rudy shoved a book at me instead; a photo album. "Sit down and look at this. I'll bring the water."

It was no use, I didn't try to argue; I sank down in the wing-back chair and the two tall girls came and stood shyly behind it, looking over my shoulder as I turned the pages.

Their baby pictures, snapshots of vacations, the grim isolated South. Several times a year Roxy goes home to her mother, who runs a gas station. In some of the photos I noticed a beautiful sturdy blond child with fat pouting cheeks and built like the baby Hercules. I asked Roxy who it was.

"Oh, that's the little daughter Rooty brung me." Rudy had found the child abandoned in a hotel room; he knew how she'd be shuffled about if he turned her over to the welfare people, so he took her home for Roxy to take care of her. In due time the mother showed up and got the child back.

Now the girls had sidled up on the arms of the chair, turning pages for me, showing me their school pictures. "Guess which one is me." The whole class lined up in the gym on wooden benches, hands folded in laps—just the way we used to do it. The same grins with the teeth missing. Only now the pictures come in color, and the girls giggled and squealed as I pointed to their faces.

"Hey, lookit—you wanna see Phoebe's report card?" Harriet said, waving the long manila envelope at me.

"Hey! No fair! Gimme that!" says Phoebe, snatching for it. I guess she's no scholar. So they started fighting, thumping and yelling. I was ready to leave, but Rudy insisted on taking me for a tour of the basement. His tall figure stooping ahead of me down the narrow steps.

As high as the ceilings are upstairs, they are that low in the basement. Rudy moved ahead of me in his slow wading way, his hands in his pockets, looking back over his shoulder; his head diving down and ducking the pipes.

I had seen it all before: the laundry room with washer and dryer; the storage room with the kids' new bikes; his own retreat—an overstuffed rocker and an old-fashioned floor lamp with a scorched parchment shade. I don't suppose he ever really uses the place. The basement is dry enough but dingy, raw cement. Rudy's eyes kept wandering, grazing all about, as if he had forgotten what he was looking for. His elbows shrugged and flopped against his sides. I was struck with the aimlessness of his wide back.

There was a workshop; but the high, rough-hewn bench, the rough shelves, were bare, except for an ashtray filled with stubbed-out butts. I wondered who had been standing in the corner, furiously smoking. "I don't know how to do nothing, so I don't use it," Rudy said, humbly, looking idly about with his hand on the light string. He ducked his head under the door as we went out.

Against the wall stood a bookcase lined with corrugated packages of light bulbs. If you pay your electric bill in person, you get them free. They caught his eye.

"You need light bulbs? Here, take some light bulbs," he said, catching at my sleeve. "What do you need? Forties? Sixties? Hundreds? They're all here; take what you want."

Turning over packages, examining them. "You need bigger ones? Here—here's one-fifty. Here's two hundred." I didn't want to take any light bulbs home with me on the bus, but he seemed very anxious for me to take some. "Soft lights? Three-way? You like pink ones? We'll get a bag upstairs." He piled the weightless packages up on me. I held out my arms.

Roxanne wanted Rudy to take her to Osco's—they had a sale on yarn. When I got into the car I saw that we had a stowaway: the little boy, squeezed between my mother's skirts and my grandmother's green coat—hiding himself, his feet sticking straight up in their dark thick-soled shoes. But before Roxy even stuck her face in, his smooth brown head popped up:

"Hi, Mommy! Hi, Mommy! Hi, Mommy!" he piped, poking his chin over the front seat and grinning up through his glasses with crazy cockeyed charm.

My grandmother peered round, large-faced in her babushka. I could see they were a little put out with me, wondering what had taken so long. "What have you got in the bag?"

"Light bulbs," I said.

I was feeling very sad. I think maybe it was the light bulbs. They made me want to cry. Once again I was looking at the back of Rudy's neck; thick, remote. For he is remote—my uncle is a blunt and mysterious man to me. His life flows in another direction; I shall never understand it. And yet I felt closer to him than to anyone I had seen all day. I felt that he had been trying to give me some message about his life; I sensed its powerlessness—but it moved me. Rudy and I are both outsiders, as far as the family is concerned. Out of the mainstream. And we are made of the same raw material: even this unexpected surge of feeling for him was an obstinate, unpredictable force. I was wondering what role such forces must have played in my life. It always feels depleting to make these self-discoveries. Anyway, it makes a long day to go up north and see the family, and by this time I had realized that I was going to feel awfully tired when I finally got home— washed out, weary, let down, empty. Blue. Yes, very blue.

TO THE COUNTRY

It just so happens that my mother's oldest and dearest friend, Little Bertha, lives on a farm not ten miles from the summer cottage where my sons and I are staying in the country—and I haven't seen her in fifteen years. At least. My father can't be dragged out to visit the Elliotts again for love nor money. My mother says he's still angry because he loaned Little Bertha's brother Bucky a few hundred dollars many years ago and never got it back. That's no surprise; everyone knows Bucky robbed his own mother. Actually they say he made her mortgage the house in exchange for favors a mother shouldn't ask. "So who tells you to go lending money to a crook like Bucky Klugman?" my mother will say. "You did," my father says. "Aren't you always telling me what to do?" "Since when do you ever listen to *me?*"

And they're off and running. Cheek to cheek.

I'd like to get a look at this Bucky, but he'll never show his face in Chicago again. Anyway, it's just an excuse; the truth is, there never was a time when my father didn't gripe about going out to see Little Bertha and Mark Elliott.

My father is a big, powerful man, almost inordinately strong, very handy. There's nothing he can't fix—or break, as the case may be. So wherever he goes, people always have something for him to do: "Wait till Sam comes." They seem to sit around helplessly, pending his arrival. He even used to get calls in the middle of the night, like a country doctor; emergencies: a car stalled on the road, water pipes bursting in the basement and no one knows how to shut it off, someone in the john and the lock got stuck. It was nothing unusual. My father would zip up his pants and spit in the sink and off he'd go to the rescue.

But there was no end to the work at the Elliotts'. They regularly seemed to be starting from scratch, nailing up chicken coops in muddy back yards. Peg and Lynn were about the same age as my sister Slim and me; but no children of theirs were going to grow up in the city. They were determined to make a big break, become farmers, lead the country life.

This new farm is only the latest in a long series, beginning with that first, half-finished place in the sticks. Mark and Bertha both held down outside jobs—old Mrs. Elliott lived with them and kept house—and they were on the go from morning till night. They were building the house and the barn and their chickens were succumbing to a million diseases. You'd find poultry stretched in the mud like corpses hanging upside down in the butcher's window. Little Bertha would seize them by their scaly reptile feet, whirl them round and round her head and let fly at the trash heap. She wasn't much bigger than I was then, and she seemed fearless to me: they were dead dead dead. At the look in their glassy eyes my heart iced over.

The Elliotts were having a hard time of it. But I didn't notice it then; I thought a hard time was what you were supposed to have. And they kept my father busy from the minute he walked in the door. Hammering roofs, blasting tree stumps, mending fences. All in a day's work for Mark; but for my father it was supposed to be a day *off*. Besides, he hated the country. Not the outdoor type. It wasn't his dream. He'd mutter and grumble and blame my mother all the way home. The back of his neck red as a brick from the sun.

My father is nothing if not a man to carry a grudge (he has "no use for" me, either), and he hasn't forgotten that Mark almost talked him into voting for Wendell Willkie. But I think the real reason he seems so reluctant to have anything much to do with the Elliotts any more is that their lives have become very different from his. Mark and Bertha have succeeded, in spite of all; they're farmers now—they have escaped the city. The transformation is complete. They vote Republican, attend church, go square-dancing on alternate Fridays (how corny can you get?). And I gather they don't get into Chicago very often nowadays. Over the phone, Bertha was still full of some wedding they had been to the last time—a big event. "Don't let me forget, now. Be sure and remind me to tell you all about that wedding."

I get the strangest feeling driving through this Indiana farmland. The fields lie flat under cultivation, the trees seem stunted by distances. Then you come upon a rise in the road; you can't see beyond, the sun is striking the side of some lone whitewashed barn. And all at once the illusion is complete. A conviction. You're not inland at all; you're at the edge of the ocean. About to confront it, begin the descent to the wave-battered coast. The light is strong and solitary. You can even smell the salt water. People from the Midwest are crazy for the sea.

The two white houses sit out side by side, practically right on top of the highway; nothing else around but wires and posts and the white line on the blacktop disappearing over the crest of the hill. Lynn and the three granddaughters live next door; easy enough to tell the houses apart. A tire swung from shady branches in front of the big old place; the kids' wagons and bikes leaned about the yard, and an Irish setter pup with its red coat rippling like prairie grass started whining and licking at the fence when it heard the car.

The other house appeared to be still under construction. Black-tar insulation, sprawling rolls of chicken wire, the grass muddy and trampled down like coconut matting. Glazier's marks still scribbled on the windows. In other words, it was Mark and Bertha's house; like all the rest of their houses: I would have known it in a dream.

Inside, the same story. Even the furniture was the same as it had always been—Sears, Roebuck Early American: spinning wheels, coffee tables, tie-back chairs. Rockers, hutches, red rock maple. Though it seemed the furniture was new, and I was not rising to the occasion; for Little Bertha had to prompt me—looking up at me sideways: "I was glad about the rug."

It's because she's so short, she seems precocious; peering up at you perkily, her head to one side, her mother-of-pearl frames tilting inquisitively. Like a curious child. And she talks a mile a minute, doesn't have time to catch her breath. The words rush out with such force you wonder how come they don't knock her right over. I remember how vigorously she used to scatter the feed—the hens in the barnyard scratching and flapping, their plucky tails taking off in all directions. They seemed in a great hurry to get out of her way.

Mark and Bertha have gone back to their first love; the new farm is devoted entirely to the production of laying hens, 36,000 of them in two long white windowless barracks. The slitted air vents gush and flutter. The farm looks like a small factory, with all its towers and power lines; all their acres are in corn for chicken feed. Not the tender sweet corn, white, almost transparent, wispily bearded, with even, pearly beads. These stalks thrust forth coarse flourishing ears, all scrambled and spotted and growing like wild. We could hear them rustling. There is a pond, a rectangular trough; you can see the teeth marks of the machinery that bit it out of the earth. A brown duck family skimmed its still surface; crows hung themselves on the hatrack of a dead naked tree. Flies snapped. Fields stirred in the sun.

Mark was in the chicken house, immunizing. He strode out in baggy overalls, square, true-jawed as ever, a red bandanna knotted round his neck, stripping off his thick rubber gloves to shake hands. His rimless specs flashed. Right away I had a mental picture of him giving injections—reaching into the straw, feeling under warm flustered feathers (the way we used to, hunting for eggs), rubbing alcohol swabs on downy white breasts. But of course things aren't done that way, not on the scale of a modern chicken farm. Everything is automated, mechanized, industrialized. The vaccine is in high-pressure tanks, sprayed into the air.

Almost immediately, Jacob, my younger son, made some remark about the cost of living going up.

"Well, now, that's only relative," Mark began, settling his cap on his graying head, with its scraped, clean jaw. First thing in the morning, in the farm dark, you used to hear the most God-awful grinding whining and squeaking—Mark, cranking the handle of his razor-blade sharpener. Without further prompting, he launched into a speech that sounded just as familiar.

About growing up the sole support of his family, a widowed mother and unmarried sisters . . . About how they were poor, but always had enough to eat . . . About how you're not really rich if you haven't got self-reliance . . . About how it was the *standard* of living that had gone up, not the *cost*—for your real needs, your basic needs, are always the same . . . How that was what was wrong with the country today . . .

It was too sudden, a little embarrassing. We stood on the heated doorstoop, listening; flies, glittering in their mail, clung to the gravelly trenches of chicken manure. Little Bertha had lowered her glance as soon as he got started. She blinked and gazed behind her big white-trimmed specs. If *I* was well-acquainted with Mark's speech, she must have heard it a thousand times.

It was this rock-ribbed conservatism of Mark's that used to get my father's goat—a factory laborer himself, a union battler. I can remember him bundling up to march off to the picket lines: two or three jackets, a couple of caps, scarves, earmuffs on his head—padded against the cold and the baseball bats. He looked like the old lady at the newsstand with her apron full of change and her cracked red hands. In his thick-clustered hair there was a small worn patch where a rock beaned him; another scar on his back, where he'd been stabbed. My father wasn't imagining things. And yet at this moment Mark reminded me utterly of him. The real impetus for this lecture—the true nerve that had been touched—was one thing they had in common. It was Mark's longing for male companionship. Someone to talk to. Something I have seen so often in my father. Mark is surrounded by women, has always, come to think of it, been surrounded, outnumbered by them. And now here were the two alert, handsome boys—eyes alight amidst sweaty thickets of hair—listening to him with upturned faces.

A steady muttering hum came from the exhaust fans of the chicken houses.

Twenty thousand chickens under one roof, without light or breeze. The air was suffocating; it snuffed your breath out. You could see white feathers stirring in dim wire cages. Row upon row, in long tiers, dark narrow aisles. They were keeping up a racket in their cracked bird voices, fussing and clucking, little chicken motors. A continuous stifled protest, a sort of treadmill of dissent.

The conveyor belts moved silently.

The birds spend all their lives in these cages; they never go outside. Ideally, they never touch the ground. They are fed by conveyor belts, watered by conveyor belts; eggs are collected on conveyor belts. The latest installation had been another belt, to haul away the manure we had seen piling up outside. Next—since one mechanical innovation begets the need for another—the manure will be chugged directly to the mill. Now it is being spread over the fields for fertilizer; then it will be ground up with the corn and fed back to the chickens.

Here and there a hen pecked tamely in the aisles, feebly almost, its red wattles trembling. Others roosted motionless, swooning under the stacks. The birds get no food or water at liberty—can't last more than twenty-four hours if they fly the coop. So someone has to go around at night, collecting all the strays and putting them back in their cages.

Bertha was rattling off all this information, parts and prices, like a mail-order catalogue. She always sounds as if she's reciting some lesson learned by heart. Her head tucked to one side, her fists clenched. In her gym shoes and ankle socks, no taller than her own grandchildren. All the profits are plowed right back into the farm, the largest in these parts. But they are on the verge of bankruptcy, the lip of ruin. . . . Everything in hock, mortgaged to the hilt; the egg business in a slump, the cost of farm equipment sky-rocketing . . . At that very moment disease was raging on the West Coast, flocks by the hundreds of thousands being exterminated, farmers wiped out . . . . An ice storm last winter had paralyzed the county, the power lines down. They carried buckets of water, feed, twenty-eight straight hours . . . prison wardens.

In other words, it was the same old story; the old continuous struggle, the day-to-day hand-to-mouth existence.

"Excuse me, and maybe I shouldn't ask this," Jacob began. I knew what was coming: his black eyes were clicking back and forth like the beads of an abacus, adding up all these figures in his head. "But how much do you think all this cost you?"

"You'll have to ask Father," Bertha said quickly.

Old Mother Elliott used to put on a spread like nobody's business; her table was literally heaped with food: hills, valleys —her own churned butter, hot biscuits to melt it, vegetables green from the garden, raspberries black from the bush. Her whipped potatoes were out of this world—not to mention her canning and preserves. She was a clean, smooth-cheeked old lady who always smelled crisp·and fresh. I don't know about the end. She had died a few years back, an uncomplaining invalid in an upstairs room. Little Bertha took care of her, driving home on her lunch hour. Bertha has never been the domestic type. She has worked all these years; now it's on the assembly line at a factory in South Bend, planting circuits in digital computers. You see a lot of aproned farm wives cashing their pay checks on Fridays in the supermarket. "It takes two working to live."

Everything on the table, with its Sunday company cloth, the paper napkins folded tricorner under the forks, was from the grocer's shelves; convenience foods, packaged, canned, frozen. Diet soda and lo-cal dressings. I had a sense of something diminished as we scraped out our chairs.

The packaged bread was still frozen stiff from the freezer, and Lynn's carrot-topped twins—sitting at the card table with napkins under their chins, wide spaces in their teeth—were warming the slices tenderly between their hands as we passed the plate.

Peg, the older daughter, was the one I used to play with as a child; but it turns out that Lynn is the one who is my age. People always said she had a "heart-shaped" face; and there it was—just like a valentine. Grave gray eyes, pointed chin. The first day the family moved onto a real farm at last—horses, cows, tractors, the rough mangled roads of the country—Lynn fell out of the hayloft and broke both her arms. The next year she fell out of her bunk bed and broke them both again. So I remember her best as up to her elbows in bent plaster casts.

But in the meantime Peg and Lynn were learning to ride horses, to can, to bake, to sew. They belonged to Girl Scouts, went to Sunday school, showed prize animals at state fairs. They were all-round 4-H champions. They rose in darkness; pulled on rubber boots to go off to their chores, wading in slippery barnyard manure. The big, soft-eyed, baggy cows, scarcely bothering to twitch their ears or glance behind them, stiffened their tails and shot out more. They talked in clear rising voices of mating, sires, dams and foals, and actually got to watch the whole thing. (I was always being told to "just look away for a minute" when we went to the zoo. Once,

41

driving through an alley, our headlights happened to pick out the figure of a man standing and urinating against a wall. The stream was hot; the bricks were darkening. Quick as a wink my mother pulled my face to her breast and covered my eyes with her hand. As you can see, the facts of life were pretty remote. Or, as my father liked to call it, "The Rude Awakening.") Mark and Bertha were getting their wish; their girls really were growing up on a farm. My sister and I were growing up in a more disorderly fashion; not to say haphazard. And I could never get it straight, what the fourth H stood for.

Oddly enough, we also lived in a house—for that time and place, a most unusual circumstance. Practically unheard of. Most of my school friends—whose fathers were chiropodists, dry cleaners, bookies and jewelers—lived in cramped flats with Murphy beds in the living rooms. They had charge plates at Carson's and Marshall Field's. To me that seemed a mark of high civilization; unattainable; like speaking French or playing the violin.

Jews had been pressing west since the days of Hull House and Maxwell Street, and could not press much farther. We were west of Pulaski Road (a.k.a. Crawford Avenue) and within a mile of the city limits, the stalwart suburbs of Cicero and Berwyn. Here and there, amidst the big brick apartment buildings, with their canyon-like courtyards, and the stone-fronted three-flats with heavy masonry steps, were small, neat, narrow houses; pointed roofs, painted porches; fenced yards, flower beds. Aluminum siding in patterns of herringbone or Harris tweed. Long flights of wooden stairs. The ground floors submerged, below street level, in the style of fifty, sixty years ago. Actually it was the sidewalks themselves that had risen; in the summer they were black under the mulberry trees. These were the dwellings of the original Bohemian settlers.

Missionaries dropped by regularly, Watchtowers in either

eye. It was embarrassing to get stopped on streetcorners and have little pamphlets shoved into your hand: "Take this home. Hide it under your pillow. Read it at night. Don't let your mama see." There was something exceptional about our position. Even our house seemed in between—squeezed on one side by Zeid's, a regular *Kesselgarten,* with tiers and tiers of rickety back porches, strung with squealing clotheslines; and, on the other, by Kovarik's—the oldest, the best-kept house on the block. Mr. Kovarik hated unions and swept his sidewalk —these things seemed to go together—after he mowed the lawn, little green whiskers of grass. Mrs. Kovarik shopped on Pulaski Road; but my mother shopped on Crawford *Avenoo.*

Our house was the famous eyesore of the neighborhood.

My father—the fixer—loved to surround himself with broken things, things that needed his attentions. Now that I think of it, it was a rural scene; houses like this you see from the railroad tracks. At least one on the outskirts of every small town. The fence sags, the gate dandles from its hinges; the steps need paint; the very grass is rusted. Strips of plastic film flutter over the windows winter and summer. These folks keep junk as others keep pigs and goats. Drums, barrels, baby buggies; empty gasoline cans of every description; bicycle frames without wheels, or wheels without frames—take your pick. Tires, inner tubes, wringer-washers with deep round tubs. (An abandoned refrigerator is always a nice touch, but they get a bad press.) You see boards, bricks, cinder blocks, ditches, sand piles, all over the place: evidence of a do-it-yourself project which the Lord in His infinite wisdom has seen fit to leave uncompleted. There will be at least one vicious-looking dog, barking its head off, lunging up on its hind legs—practically strangling itself at the end of a rope.

Nowadays, of course, such a collection would be bound to include a television tube or two, a power mower or motorcycle or snowmobile, keeping up with the times, the totems of a reckless civilization. My father, according to my mother, had "all the time in the world." On a twenty-five-foot city lot, his space was limited. This must be how come he never acquired the badge of honor, the purple heart—the stripped-down truck chassis overturned in the front yard.

You may be sure this was a fairly constant topic of conversation.

When was he going to fix the faucets, the light switches? (You had to screw bulbs on and off by hand and get your fingers burned.) Why couldn't our radio be made to work, the same as anyone else's? (On Sunday evenings, with much muttering and demanding to know "who the aitch had been fooling around with it" my father would unscrew the back of the cabinet, fiddle with tubes, touch a few wires together, and produce the voice of Walter Winchell: "Good evening, Mr. and Mrs. North and South America . . .") When was my father going to take a look at my mother's washing machine, since he had just repaired the next-door neighbor's? Hadn't she been pleading with him for months? (My mother never asked; she *pleaded*. In the same way, Slim and I didn't exactly speak; we only *claimed*.) Why couldn't the girls have bikes, if my father—a very popular guy—had put together bikes, from spare parts, for half the kids on the block?

"A prophet is without honor in his own country," my father would say, frowning over the crossword puzzle, without looking up. He always worked the crossword puzzle at the dinner table, sharpening his pencil with quick curly strokes of his penknife and sticking it behind his ear, in his thick curly hair. This was how come he spoke in dashes and aitches and absentmindedly asked for the s-a-l-t.

Well, how about throwing out the garbage?

In the back yard my father kept his dogs, a pitch-black pair with hides smooth as tar and chests shaped like gun barrels.

They were of a litter that had been destroyed, the father turned killer. My father brought them home in a box.

I happened to be lying on the couch under a blanket, a wet washcloth across my eyes, a thermometer in my mouth—*claiming* some childhood illness or other. A smell of Vicks Vapo Rub; a dimness of drawn shades; a steaming glass of tea.

My father looked at me with a gleam in his eye, hugging the carton under his arm. It was moving; he had to hold the top down with both hands. "Puppies," he said, stepping back. The lid popped open. Out rolled two stir-crazy dogs, stumbling and tumbling over each other. You could hear their claws clattering like dice. Their tails were lashing. They came crashing over the table, splashed the tea, smashed the glass, knocked the thermometer out of my mouth, yanked off my blankets with a wrench of their jaws, and sank their teeth into my legs. I thought of sharks. Then they squatted down— looking contrite—and did their business in the middle of the floor.

After this they stayed in the back yard—had the run of the place—and my mother tossed them their scraps out the back window. They galloped round and round, digging up everything in sight, their tongues hanging out like slices of meat. Trophies of flesh. There but for the grace of God go I. This was how come my father had to throw out the garbage. Mr. Kovarik complained about "property values."

My sister Slim was a freer spirit. She'd cheat before your very eyes at cards. She liked to throw off all her clothes, climb out the bedroom window, and run around on the steep porch roof stark naked. Mrs. Kovarik's fat white chow, Chummy, was getting on; had a cataract in one eye and roving habits; and she used to watch for him from behind her curtains. Whenever she spotted Slim at it again, her fat white bottom bouncing up and down on the gutter pipes—which my father was still getting around to repairing—all the world knew how loose they were—she would call the police. Or better yet, the fire department. The hook-and-ladder would come wailing up, engines shuddering, and firemen leaping off the sides in their big gloves and boots, axes slung on their shoulders.

After the war began the wholesale migration of whites out of, blacks into, the West Side of Chicago; completed sometime in the mid-fifties. (Some day there ought to be plaques of bronze all over the city—the kind you see in scenic or historic areas—commemorating these landmarks and battle zones.) If I wanted to, I could probably fix the final hour, name the exact date on which there were no longer any Jews left in all of Lawndale. That had to be the day we moved. My father was a hard man to budge.

One night my mother woke to find a man bending over her bed. She could hear my father downstairs in the kitchen, stirring the spoon in his coffee cup. He was awfully fond of sugar. "Why, he's let someone get in and he doesn't even know it." She gave a feeble cry and tried to sit up.

My father rushed toward the stairs and snapped on the light.

At once the figure began to glow. He appeared to be a Hindu; he was little and frail, with nothing on but a turban and loincloth. She could see his ribs, distinctly outlined—a pale-green glimmer, like the spark of cigar butts or fireflies. He hesitated, wavered, and faded out of sight.

My mother said she had been hearing the same stealthy footsteps creeping up the stairs for years—only they had never made it to the top before.

"It's an Omen," my father said. "Looks like it's time we moved. If the house is going to be haunted."

Naturally there were a few embarrassing questions.

"When are your folks coming out to see us again, it's been so long?" Mark and Bertha wanted to know. "And your sister Slim—we used to get such a kick out of her. What's her husband do?" (He locks himself in the bathroom and sits there in the dark till you leave, that's what he does. What my father calls "a character.")

But the conversation over the meal was mostly about farmers' dogs getting killed on the highway, a regular occurrence. Traffic has increased on these back roads; Lynn says she's afraid to let the girls ride their bikes. It's ever since they opened up I-94 and I-80. The green signs are everywhere. They used to say you could hear the corn growing; now you hear the truck tires, punching out the miles.

Every once in a while a pickup truck hurtled past and drummed the dishes on the table.

The very pictures hanging all about us were the same; oil originals, they had belonged to Mark's grandfather. Nature scenes, woods, mountains, waterfalls. The thick raised brush strokes shone darkly in heavy gilt frames. I used to think the largest was supposed to be best, because it was biggest.

Mark noticed me looking.

"Guess I ought to take 'em in and get 'em appraised one of these days," he said, raising shining specs to the wall. "Maybe one of the artists died and got famous."

That was the joke he always used to make.

Jacob spoke up. "I hope you don't mind my asking. But how much would you say all of this is worth?"

"Well, now, that's hard to say." Mark tucked his chin over his plate. "I did most of the work myself, you know."

"Just an estimate," Jacob said tactfully.

"I was going to tell her about the *wedding,*" Bertha chimed in.

Mark looked up. "What wedding was that, Mother?"

"Why, the wedding we went to in *Chicago.*" She sounded rather hurt.

That did it. All you have to do is say "Chicago." At once the conversation turned to crime.

The streets of Michigan City and South Bend aren't safe any more, deserted after dark; business districts are dead. People go to huge outlying shopping centers, which have sprung up like oil rigs on the highways. Even social life has moved there: restaurants, cinemas, bowling alleys, cocktail lounges. Things have started happening which never used to occur in this part of the world before. Bodies locked in trunks, shootouts in gas stations, brutal murders which make even the Chicago papers —so you can imagine the big splash in the local press, with the news of church bake sales and false-alarm fires.

This is not the usual stuff: suicide pacts and exploding gas heaters.

There was the woman who went shopping in Kalamazoo. Her car was abandoned in the parking lot. A few days later a hitchhiker spotted a grisly blood-smeared infant sitting at the side of the road, prattling and pointing into the bushes. There they found the mother's body.

In Cassopolis, a man and wife were slain in bed—tortured, their throats slit. Once again, a pair of toddlers were witness to their parents' murder—standing in their cribs.

I could see Lynn took an interest in this gory fare; she dramatized, pointing her finger like the infant in her story, and her great gray eyes opened wide in staring childish horror. I must confess I take an interest myself. My aunt was murdered when I was a very small child, and my cousin—her daughter —and I discovered the body. She had been strangled, her apron strings knotted so tightly round her throat that they were hidden in its flesh. We thought she was fooling. We each grabbed an arm and started dragging, pulling, to make her get up. Her hand was limp, it offered no resistance. For many years after I could remember her heavy hand pulling on me, but thought it was a dream. My cousin moved away with her father; I never saw her again.

I know that evil is a great preoccupation of our life in the city; I am used to conversations like this, I am very much aware of being a woman alone. But it surprised me to learn that it's the same in the country, that people talk about the crime, they are preoccupied with crime—and all that goes with it. Fear and violence are by-blows of our modern life. They feel this life encroaching, closing in on them.

The fear of crime is profoundly a class fear: the fear of becoming a victim, of joining the ranks of the expendables— those spewed up by the system; of offering your neck to be butchered and slaughtered and laying yourself down with the rest. I realized the extent to which this has come to pass when we were pulling into the city one day, getting off at the Illinois Central station on Fifty-fifth Street. The little red train from the country arrived at the rush hour. It was drizzling, passengers were alighting from cars heading in the opposite direction, coming out of the Loop. Steamy plastic raincoats, umbrellas, tired lines straggling toward the gates. The stairs were wet and muddy. The tracks are elevated here, tumbleweed blows off the railroad ties, down the steep embankments, rolls sweeping end over end through the ranks of housing projects.

Something was wrong. You could see the crowd halting ahead at the very bottom of the stairs. A snarl, a backup, something blocking the way. Two youths were killed, shot in the head at this station one recent evening while it was still light. So my first thought was "Oh, no." But what it was was a cat. A large, bluish, white-spotted animal lying on its side, all four paws stretched out. At first glance it appeared to be dead; then I saw its dark quavering gaze. It seemed to be trying to raise its head, glance backward over its shoulder. "Not for long," someone said.

As we went out past the gates I could see through the bars the last of the passengers still gathered round, looking down at the cat, helpless to express their concern. And as a matter of fact it is a rarity to see an animal on the city streets in this

49

condition. People in a bad way you see all the time. You give them a wide berth.

All at once, through the bars, the cat became a man before my very eyes. I saw him lying on his side in the same stiff way, trying to lift his head up and look behind him over his shoulder with the same quaking motion. He was a black man in a black raincoat, with a bottle in his pocket; his fingers reaching, outspread. Was he supposed to be drunk? Having an attack of some sort? Had someone pushed him? Was he wounded? Had he stumbled and fallen? His eyes were shining and shivering like muddy pools of water. And the heels, umbrellas, were tap-tapping around him, passengers quickening their gait, avoiding his eyes.

Dawn, the oldest granddaughter, suddenly jumped up, pointing to the window. Her chair toppled backward, her fork dropped with a clatter. "Flaming Molly got out! Flaming Molly got out!" Her hair was about the shade of the Irish setter's, and her little gold locket was rising and falling on her chest.

Sure enough, the big red dog came streaking past the window, its head between its paws and its tail like a brush fire. *Oh, no. Not again. How'd that happen?* Everyone was in an uproar. The twins shrieked and tore their napkins. I gathered that Flaming Molly was not long for this world.

Frank and Jake, all flushed with the excitement of the chase, ran out with Dawn to catch the dog. (Have I mentioned that she is a raving beauty?) Their footsteps jolted the bare unnailed boards of the porch. In no time at all the meal had disbanded; Lynn marched the little ones home across the lawn, Mark went back to his chores. I started to clear the table.

"Never mind all that," Little Bertha whispered, quickly wiping down her hands on her apron. "Now's my chance to tell you all about that wedding."

We sat side by side on the sofa, the scrapbook open across our knees. I saw I was in for a fairly lengthy and detailed description, not to say history. How many years Mark and Bertha had known the bride's family; what good time they had made driving into Chicago; how they got lost, circling all around, looking for the church. . . . Okay, okay; so they finally made it. The organ was playing, ushers were taking guests by the elbows, leading them down the aisle to their pews. Programs were being distributed. *Programs?* Apparently this was to be one of those do-it-yourself scripts: a lot of quotations from Kahlil Gibran and Rod McKuen substituted for the vows and holy scriptures.

All of a sudden the lights went out, the church fell silent; a white movie screen dropped down in place of the altar. Onto it there flashed—a naked toothless baby on a bearskin rug. The groom. Over a microphone came a voice out of the darkness: the groom's mother, telling the story of his life. Accompanied by slides. The groom's first teeth, his baby shoes —dipped in plaster. The groom in a cowboy hat with strings round his neck and his little legs dangling from the back of a pony in Lincoln Park Zoo. And so forth and so on. Talk about history. Then the same with the bride. Her childish scrawls; her striped spelling papers with gummed red stars. She had had corrective surgery on her hip as a child, and even this was not overlooked—there she was on the screen, smiling and struggling in her casts and crutches.

Several of the groom's musical compositions were played on the guitar, and the bride's poetry was read aloud. It was announced that there would be a display immediately following the reception line—the newlyweds' arts and crafts.

I was stunned. I had been expecting a tale of hippies and flower children, bearded boys and braless girls, but what would you call *this?* What could you make of it? You go to a ceremony, and you get an exhibition. I had to say *something*

—Little Bertha was looking up at me expectantly, her head perched to one side.

"It sounds like the bride and groom have a lot in common," I said.

"Yes. I'm sure they'll have a wonderful life." Her shoulders heaved a small sigh. "But I'm just not doing it justice," she said, shaking her head. "It's too hard to remember it all, it's been such a long time."

"Say, when was this wedding anyhow?"

Bertha flipped through the pages. "June fifteenth, nineteen s— Why, that's four years ago!"

She clapped the book shut on her knees and lifted her face wistfully, clucking her tongue. "My, my—how time flies," she said.

Let me tell you about this part of the country. At one time the southeastern shores of Lake Michigan thronged and thrived with summer resorts. My friends spent the entire summer vacation at Gottlieb's, Gettel's, Fiddelman's, in towns with names like South Haven, Benton Harbor, Union Pier. The towns still have the same names, but they don't sound the same to me. These were places of summer romance: they went to meet boys; they talked about Gary, Barry, Terry all winter. (The names of choice in my generation.) I didn't know anything else about life in the country, and I didn't care, either. I didn't grow up on the West Side of Chicago for nothing. I had no use for the outdoors; it made no difference to me—all I knew of nature was what dropped from the trees. What were those shiny, sticky things like black bean pods? Where did they come from? And the soft chains we used to call "caterpillars"? And what about the leaves? What did you call them? I never learned their names.

My proletarian family did not go in for that sort of thing. When I was very small we used to make our annual expedition to the beach—something of an ordeal. You took the Roosevelt Road car to the end of the line, forty-two blocks—Chicago blocks, long ones, and it ground to a halt at every other corner—and then you walked another mile with the blankets and Thermos bottles. The bathhouses smelled of slimy timber; you had to race through them quickly, ducking the sniper spray of icy-cold showers. I wore rubber beach shoes, a rubber cap, a suit with no top(!). My father would scoop out a hole in the sand and crouch down in it—his thighs as thick around as tree stumps in his Charles Atlas trunks—trying to shrink and make himself look smaller, while someone snapped our picture with our black box camera. Otherwise his head and hairy shoulders would get lost above the rest.

On the long rides home Slim always fell asleep.

The streetcar was crowded; we had to split up. My father sat all the way up front with my fat little sister sprawled in his lap, his own big head nodding and dozing. It fell on his chest. My mother and I found seats in the back. The aisle got more and more crowded, people swayed from the straps; the car went slower and slower—dragging on, clanging, complaining. The long-drawn-out whine twanged the heart.

But it seemed to me that this was the way I spent most of my life: waiting. Waiting in buses, streetcars, automobiles; waiting on benches, stairways, laps, knees. Waiting in crowds, doctors' offices, clinics; waiting on beds heaped with rough coats at family parties. Waiting in the dark. Waiting alone. Waiting for nothing. This was the real tyranny of childhood. I wanted to be grown up and done with it—done with waiting—just so no one ever again would have such power over me.

I laid my head against the back of the seat and my gaze drifted toward the window. Suddenly I heard my mother let out such a shriek that every head turned the whole length of the car.

"Sam! She's asleep!"

That was *me.* I was looking at her too. Instantly I shut my eyes, dropped my head to my shoulder. And I pretended to be asleep (to be on the safe side) all the rest of the way home. My father had to carry both of us slung from his back.

So how should I have known that I would grow up with such strange longings, such a passion for "nature"? That I should have been asking questions all along? That I would want to tuck myself away in the country and learn the names of things?

The boys and I are sharing this summer cottage with a couple; we use it during the week, they come out on weekends. An ideal arrangement, except I'm sore half the time: someone uses your last clean towel, or eats up the leftovers you were counting on finding in the refrigerator. Or, departing, my friends go to great pains to lock up the place—draw all the windows, shut it like an oven—and forget to throw out their rotting garbage. It leaks all over and stinks to high heaven. The whole house swarms with fruit flies.

Unwelcome thoughts darken my door, enter my soul. They walk right in, make themselves at home. I could be put in prison for thoughts like those.

But I don't have to go into explanations. The case is simple. I'm jealous, possessive about the house—I don't want to share it. I don't want to share anything. I want to pack up my children and have a place of our own. This is my most persistent fantasy. I even subscribe to farm realty catalogues so I can read all about the Sportsman's Hideaways, Handyman's Specials, Sacrifices to Settle Estates. "The Land Remains." (It occurs to me that these catalogues are my equivalent of the rural scenes on the walls of the Elliotts' house—calendar paintings.)

It doesn't have to be the best place in the world, nothing special, no castle, no dream house. Riding along, I'll spot some austere and isolated shack—a roof, a porch, a weed-strewn path—and I'm ready to love it. To spring out of the car, fling my arms around it, twine myself, cling to it, sink my roots deep. If it will only *be mine.*

Too bad you can't feel that way about people.

Zimmerman's falls squarely into the category of Handyman's Specials. Mrs. Zimmerman and her husband staked out this land over forty years ago, and once owned all the cottages you see around here. Her husband is dead now, as she's sure to mention on every possible occasion, anytime she corners you—a tiny woman with frizzy gray hair and great big tiger eyes, magnified, welling up to the very rims of her thick glasses.

"My husband is dead now, you know."

"Yes, yes, I know."

The tenants try to evade the old landlady's tediousness. Though it's easy enough to understand. She feels diminished. She is not what she once was. This is not the truth about her —not the whole truth.

Most of the cottages belong to black families now, who live in them themselves and do not rent them out, and have put a lot of work into their places. Paint, shingles, cinder blocks; concrete patios, chain-link fences. Roofs straddled by TV antennas like Texas Towers—it still takes a lot of power out this way to get a picture. The rest—what's left of Zimmerman's Lakefront Villas (they're not on the lakefront, that goes without saying; you can't even see Lake Michigan from here)—are merely six or seven of the most leaning, the most dependent, the most run-down, crippled and dilapidated. It won't be so easy to get rid of *them.* Which the old lady would dearly love to do, all right; she longs to soar away and be free. Help is so hard to get these days.

Missus Z. swears up and down by Mrs. Hodiak, the cleaning woman, who routs the cottages out in spring. Sweeps up the curled wasp corpses, the mouse pellets, the fly-speckled newspapers laid over the furnishings like wares in a shopwindow —three-legged armchairs, sagging studio couches, dressers with stuck drawers and sourpussed mirrors. Mrs. Hodiak is stout and fearless with her mops and buckets. Her hair is like a paintbrush dipped in lampblack, white at the roots.

It was cold when we first came out and I foolishly asked how to light the rusty old heater; I've always been skittish about holding up flaming matches to hissing gas. Mrs. Hodiak without a word dropped onto all fours and crawled under the buffet. That's where the heater sits, don't ask me why. I could see her big shaved legs and gym shoes sticking out.

"Never mind, Mrs. Hodiak, please, forget it," I said, as she crouched, her heavy back wedged in, scratching matches under her thumbnails.

There was a pop, but no explosion. Nothing lighted. No gas, of course. Mrs. Zimmerman seems to be the only one left who still expects the heaters to give forth, rise and shine; the toilets to shut their noisy traps for a change and quit dripping deliriously (no more graceful fountains); the showers to do more than cough up a few drops of surly brown water, rattle their pipes and knock it off.

She seems so surprised and disappointed, in fact—the big yellow eyes sweeping up, trustingly, in her small wrinkled face —that you really hate to mention it. Like the hole in the boys' bedroom ceiling where the roof is caving in. What's the use? What can she do about it? Or the bathroom floor rotting away under the tub. The screen doors are a laugh.

"Mrs. Hodiak scrubs these cottages from top to bottom; she makes them *spotless*," the old landlady says with pride.

What it amounts to is this: Mrs. Zimmerman—by default— is a holdout, a survivor. I made it up here twenty years too late. But she still thinks someone is going to come along and take all this off her hands. And you can always tell when something's up, she's got another prospect on the hook. An old man—another ancient faithful retainer, stooped, gnarled, with a spattered cap and overalls that hang drooping from their bucklestraps—shows up, bright and early, and starts slapping white paint all over the place. He splatters the greenery.

The old guy must be stone deaf under his cap; his portable radio jumps and jangles and blares like a loudspeaker. The lawnmowers buzz, riding herd over the grass; the garbage trucks back up, groaning and grinding and gnashing their teeth. The neighbors' miniature poodles (all the neighbors own little white poodles with legs like pipe cleaners) sound off from their rhinestone-studded throats. Abused little yips and yaps. Even the woodpeckers get into the act—typing in the trees, hunt and peck; very unsystematic. In other words, life out here goes on—industriously. *And it's not supposed to.* It's supposed to stop, to hold still for us. Everyone knows that. Isn't that the proper definition of life in the country?

The tenants wish she'd leave well enough alone.

This neck of the woods has always been a Bohemian stronghold in the summertime, and it still is. The old resorts still gang up one right on top of the other: Hspuda's, Redimak's, Sixta's. The restaurants with thatched roofs and stenciled shutters; the dark little groceries where they sell shriveled sausages and heavy black bread and display all the mimeographed announcements—dances, raffles, bingo. They'll cash checks if they know you. Their strong community spirit definitely does not extend to outsiders. This is exactly the pattern the transition from white to black followed in the city—where all that dark bread comes from; husky loaves stickered with labels from bakeries in Bridgeport, Brighton, along Archer Avenue. These are the so-called ethnic neighborhoods—i.e., white working class. Inch by inch the ground is contested in classic style: you read about bricks and fire bombs hurled through windows, crosses burned on lawns, parents picketing schools. Everyone knows that Czechs, Poles, Lithuanians, Irish, are more stubborn than Jews.

At Zimmerman's, however, there are certain changes rung on these old stereotypes. Here it is the blacks who are the conventional, stable families; who own homes, who maintain them, who put up fences and fire up coals with lighter fluid on their portable grills. The whites are refugees from Hyde Park, university liberals—the other kind of Bohemians.

At seven o'clock in the morning, Mrs. Bledsoe, sitting on her screened-in porch across the way, starts to give Byron his lessons in table manners. Mrs. Bledsoe is a round, brown, smiling woman who wears turbans, great dangling earrings wriggling like bait, long colorful robes. She looks like an African ambassadress—even when she throws out the garbage, the loose tropical sleeves flowing and fluttering as she slams and bangs the lids. She takes in children from the ghetto to board in summer, so they can taste the benefits of country life. "And because I never had any of my own," she says. (She pronounces it *get-toe,* in rich penetrating tones, to let you know it's not where she's from.) The little colony can be seen traipsing down the dusty path to the lake, Mrs. Bledsoe, her buttocks swaying in her long gown, forging ahead; the children scraping along in rubber thongs, striped beach towels over their shoulders. Later their wet suits hang on the line.

Byron is the youngest, the smallest, the puniest; the skinniest, blackest legs, the biggest ears; and his belly slopes and sticks out the most. He wears a yellow beanie with something like a windmill or weather vane on top. When the others tease him (they perpetually tease him), don't let him catch the Frisbee or take his turn at bat, he chases back and forth, frantic. I see the weathercock whirling on the top of his head.

I get very maudlin about Byron's yellow beanie.

"Don't slop your oatmeal, Byron."

"What you say when you ask for something? You. Byron."

"And what you say when you get it?"

I think she slaps his hands.

The light of the young morning creeps across the dewy grass. But this is not what I bargained for when I rented a house in the country. Not the twittering of boisterous birds in the trees. It makes me cringe. I feel it is partly on my account that Mrs. Bledsoe is making Byron's life so miserable, that he keeps getting it day after day like this. And it *is* partly on my account. Her voice rises, carries, sharp as a laugh—it means to be overheard. *Byron! Byron!* The other children titter—who can blame them? A moment of freedom for them. They're not even permitted to go barefoot, Mrs. Bledsoe's so strict: "It looks trashy." Whose world does she think she's making them fit to live in?

Our porch—we took this cottage for its screened-in porch, though it's in even worse shape than the house—is full of garbage. Belle and Emile save all our trash so they can take it to the recycling center at the Bethlehem Steel plant. That is their hobby. Recycling center at Bethlehem Steel—how d'ya like the nerve? That pipe organ on the lakefront. They belong to Zero Population Growth. They own two houses and three cars. (No, make that four. I gave my car to Emile on condition that he never mention it to me again. It was the kind of car you have fantasies of abandoning; the guy who sold it to me must have thought he had died and gone to heaven when he saw a sucker like me coming, with my great big smile.)

Our refuse isn't enough for them; they go around collecting from other cabins too. Tins, jars, soda bottles, beer cans, great green jugs of Gallo and Pio Vino. The stuff is stashed all over the place. Shopping bags buckle under their loads. Stacks of Sunday papers, comics, rotogravures. Then there are the ecological experiments: piles of browning corncobs (for fuel?); rheumy watermelon rinds. Belle and Emile know how I love to throw things out, so they leave notes for me:

This is not garbage. Please save.

That's not all. I nearly forgot the dishes of dogchow, boxes of kitty litter. They have three cats and two dogs. It would be no fun driving back to Chicago with all of them in the rear seat of a rusty Volkswagen, so the cats remain with us. Large, placid, easygoing Belle, with her big hips and pale ponytail, her long teeth like a rabbit's, straps herself in, stroking the old white dog in her lap. The young dog waves its lofty tail from the window. And out pops Emile's wedge of red beard, anxiously reminding us, just one more time:

"Don't let the cats get out."

Don't let the cats get out. The cats are shy and strange and keep trying to run away. We have to shut them up whenever we attempt to leave; they hide from us, bound off, dive under the furniture. Their telltale eyes glare from dark corners.

One is black and white, fat and sleek and easy to catch. But Jacob spends a lot of time parked on his narrow haunches, lifting the edges of blankets, poking under beds—his thick shocks of bushy dark hair sticking out aft—coaxing the lean striped tabbies:

"Here, kitty kitties . . . here, kitty kitties . . ."

Frank and Jake are of an age and have always been close. Being shunted around—their father and I were divorced when they were babies—has made them closer. Frank is thirteen now, he's pulled ahead; broad-shouldered, gruff-voiced (Arf! Arf! Arf!)—almost hulking. His wrists protrude from the sleeves of his pajamas and the pants legs look as though they shrank to his ankles. Nobody notices these developments with more interest, more awe, than Jacob. "Holding Frank's hand is like holding a man's hand," he says.

Their father has married again; he has a new wife, a new

child. I wonder if the boys feel at home there. Maybe they are on their good behavior, there are things they are afraid to say? Are they only guests in his house? And isn't it the same for them with me? Mine is a makeshift sort of life; I didn't plan it that way, I just don't have all the pieces. I'm sure they notice. Do they watch out? Do they bite their tongues?

"I'm always at home where Jacob is," Frank told me.

At first the boys played with Ralphie, a big heavy shuffling good-natured kid; a cowlick, calamine lotion smeared all over his fat red cheeks. He'd gotten into some poison ivy. His hand was in a sling, taped to the wrist, the thumb in a splint—just the fingernails sticking out; a firecracker had gone off in his mitt on the Fourth of July. He limped a little, lurched to one side—an ankle twisted in a fall from a tree. The boys assured me he was just accident-prone.

Then Jacob started asking, "Hey, Ma, is it all right if we sneak off after lunch and go fishing with Ralphie? . . . Can we have permission to sneak off after dinner? Huh, Ma?"

"Sure. But who sez you have to *sneak off?*"

"Ralphie does. His mother's punishing him. He's not supposed to leave his room except to go to the toilet. But he climbs out the window."

Ralphie's mother is Gladys, a widow with an administrative job at the University; she comes out with her mother and five children. One son died in Vietnam. Gladys is a blond meaty woman with a ruddy thick-blooded face; the old mother is bony and scrawny and white as a ghost. And yet the two women are unmistakably of one flesh. It's the way they carry themselves—six feet tall, with heavy slouching shoulders, bison humps. It gives them a hangdog, defeated appearance; you can see they are used to being ineffectual.

Ralphie's "punishment" is typical; the threats fly thick and fast and no one listens to them anyway. "All right, I'm gonna leave you right here, then," I hear the old woman telling the baby, as it sits and bawls in a puddle in its diapers and pins. "You find your way back to Chicago all by yourself."

And yet it was Gladys who finally forbade Ralphie to play with my boys—because, she said, they used foul language. Then the three rosy little girls had to stop playing with their friends for the same reason. Very soon there was no one left who had not offended in this way, and Gladys's brood had no one to play with. On the beach she spreads their blanket far from the rest, and passing in the road she won't glance up, keeps her distance—humped, slouching, her feet pounding with determination, her chin hung forward with heavy pride.

You may be sure I enter into the spirit of things, narrow my eyes, set my jaw too. Hard feelings are so good for the arteries.

I was getting a patch put on a bicycle tire at the gas station on the highway. The temperature was in the nineties, the tar was melting. The light hurt your eyes. Every time a car whizzed past, shrapnel, all the signs started rattling and the colored streamers raised a dirty breeze.

The attendant came squinting up to me. He was drinking a warm Coke—the vending machine was broken. The brown liquid foamed and fizzed under his thumb.

"You see that guy that was here just now? The one in the suit and necktie. That was driving the blue panel truck."

I had noticed a truck standing at the pumps.

"Well, that's the deputy. He's got six colored boys in back he's taking up to the state prison in Jackson and they asked for a drink a water. Boy, you should of seen it. There's no windows back there, it ain't nothing but tin; I bet it was a hundred and twenty degrees sitting under that roof. The sweat was just pouring off them. They were *shining.* And the smell that was coming outta there could knock you right over.

"And the deputy," he said, shaking his head, "I seen him

go in and give 'em their water. Some job he's got, huh? I wouldn't do that if you paid me."

Something knocks off the lids of the garbage cans and digs and scratches in the middle of the night. What can it be? A fox? A masked raccoon? Everyone is secretly pleased; proud of our possession of this wild creature (we hope it's wild). It is to us what the bears are to Yellowstone, ambling in under the tent flaps and eating up the peanut butter. Ambassadors. Ah, wilderness. It's official—we're in the country. When I hear it poking, nosing around, I jump out of bed and grab my flashlight, run to the door, shining its beam into the darkness; searching searching for two points of light, the pair of eyes burning at me like taillights.

Surprise. It *is* the country. How long has it been since I smelled summer nights? At that hour, the air is so sharply pure your breath cracks; the trees are creaking overhead like old weatherbeaten barns. Mosquitoes sprinkle the grass, heavy as dew. And the Little Dipper, sparkling away up there, reminds me suddenly, forcibly of childhood . . . sitting out late on our front steps, gazing up, wondering, at those same targets strewn over the summer night. The same? So they're still up there? Belle took her class of inner-city dropouts to the planetarium, and the kids clapped politely when the stars came out.

I haven't seen this animal yet. And it occurs to me: what if it's only a rat? A cat? Escaped? One of the neighbors' toy poodles with their jeweled collars and red ribbons? (No wonder they protest so much.) Or it could be Sadie, up to her scavenging and rummaging.

Everyone knows better than to start up with Sadie—hard enough to avoid her as it is. You wake up and find her face against the screen, her hand to her forehead, peering in. An old harpy head, streaked white bangs and beetling black brows. Always twitching.

63

"Just sniffing your flowers," she says.

Sadie knows every abandoned house for miles around—she's looted them all. She prowls the woods in helmet and slicker, galoshes, thick gloves, got up for the occasion like a welder or a beekeeper.

Sadie comes trudging down the loose rickety stairs to the beach—someone's going to do himself a mischief one of these days—her rubber galoshes flopping their tongues, swathed to the chin in a conspicuously striped beach towel. Very conspicuous—it's mine. I was wondering what happened to it.

It's wonderful, though, how everyone puts up with Sadie; the price you have to pay for a little fresh air.

Gladys lives on the other side of the same duplex (all seven in two rooms), so the women have been carrying on a running feud. Naturally you hear everything through the cardboard walls, and Sadie is forever thumping on them with (I presume) her broomstick.

I was talking to Sadie in back of the white frame cottage when Gladys came charging round the bend, her head lowered, very red in the face.

"All right, Sadie, I give up, I can't take it any more. I'm here to beg you—is that what you want? Beg you to stop."

"Stop what?" says Sadie, not at all taken aback—as I was—but looking up and raising her glass to her lips. She was seated in a deck chair, drinking rosé from a shrimp-cocktail jar. All around us the smell of paint-spattered, fresh-scissored grass.

"Stop swearing at my children!"

"They swore at me first."

"Sadie. They're *children.*" Gladys was choking back tears.

"They started it, I didn't," Sadie said.

I'd never seen her so composed. She sank back calmly in the arms of the striped chair, stretched out her legs—one ankle in its rubber galosh crossed atop the other—looking up at Gladys, her black eyebrows raised above the rim of her glass.

And they weren't even twitching; her nervous tic had disappeared, stopped like a clock.

"I'm begging you, Sadie, leave us alone. What harm have I ever done you? We try to keep out of your way. I'm shushing my children all the time when you're at home. *What is it? What do you want from us? Why do you have to make my life so miserable!*"

Gladys's face was getting thicker and redder. All at once I understood—not a moment too soon, considering I'm in such a good position to appreciate—looking at her hunched shoulders, shaking angry jaws. A cornered creature, at bay. A husband dead, a son killed in the war, the children too much for her, the mother disappointed—a life of constant self-reproach. She was beside herself, leading a manless, unconsoled existence. The fear, the loneliness, managing alone. And of course pride.

Sadie smirked and sipped her pink wine.

I got up and took Gladys by the arm. "Come away, come away, Gladys," I said. "Can't you see she's enjoying this? She loves it, she thrives on it, this is what she lives for. You're no match for her. It can only hurt you."

"All I ask is a little peace," Gladys said. She had begun to cry in earnest and her big sunburned peeling shoulders were shaking. I put my arms around her, meaning to press her cheek to my shoulder. But since she's a good half foot taller than I am, that was impossible. I dropped my head on her shoulder instead.

"Why can't we have a little peace and quiet?" she cried. "Why oh why does it always have to be so hard? I come up to the country with my children to get away from all that. But it's the same here. Why do I feel like this? Why am I always so angry?"

She rocked and sobbed while I patted her on the hump, mindlessly, like burping a baby. Oh, yes. If not for Sadie, for the damned cats and the garbage and kitty litter. If Mrs. Bledsoe would just quit picking on Byron—in the tender hours of the morning at least. If only we could remove all these extra distractions . . . If if if.

And yet in spite of everything, the first thing that happens every summer is that everyone starts talking and scheming about giving it all up, moving out here altogether, living here year round. They've had it with the city—dirt, crime, crowding, corruption. To the country! To the country! It's only a matter of rearranging all the querulous details, our circumstantial lives.

So where is it, then? Where is the rightful life that is awaiting us? Where is that undiscovered territory? Where the air is clear and consciences are clean. How do we get there? How do we cut our path through this wilderness? How do we run up our flags and stake our claims? The tyranny, the tyranny of these dreams of peace and quiet.

PUBLIC
FACILITIES

The most popular volume in the branch library was the medical dictionary. You had to ask. It was kept under lock and key in a glass case. Customers coughed behind their hands, trying not to look worried about their health. As if their troubles weren't plain enough. Watery sores, hoarse whispers, swollen legs, mackerel skins. One woman who kept coming in all winter long had something the matter with her nose. A hole in it; it was being eaten away. From her nose the condition progressed to her eye. The other eye—the one you could look at—twinkled and gleamed with classified secrets. At last she began to wear a bandage. That was too much. You couldn't help wondering what this bandage must be hiding—if it was still worse. Leprosy? The first thing I would think of. Our vocabulary of suffering is so limited. Maybe that's why these people were boning up.

But a lot of good. What was the use? It could only have sounded all the alarms, aroused fresh anxieties, deeper fears. The medical dictionary came back to the desk without comment. Miss Rose, the reference librarian, would seize the germy contaminated thing and lock it up again. Lock it up and then—she couldn't help it, kindly as she was, with her loud rude voice and knocking heels—she'd trot straight to the john and scrub her hands with green soap.

I lived in the neighborhood at the time, a few blocks' walk from my job at the branch, and saw a lot of this. There is more than urban poverty in Uptown. The population is largely Appalachian, American Indian, and they bring a special rural desolation. The streaked grime—melting snow—characteristic of the bricks of Chicago in winter, can be seen here even on the faces. Mexican, Korean, black, Puerto Rican, pensioned-off Jew: they get along more or less without racial strife. To tell the truth, that's the least of their worries.

Uptown lies a few miles north of the Loop along the lakefront, so it is bounded by high rises, motel architecture, rocky breakwaters, the twinge of lights on the Outer Drive. Lake Michigan spreads its deep blue rumor. Walls of glass greet the rising sun. First thing in the morning, salesmen are out cruising the streets slowly as cops in squad cars. Same thing goes on all afternoon—Businessmen's Lunch. These are the times when the younger and prettier girls work their shift. Only the old war-horses come out at night. Bloated bare legs blue with bruises, plucked like turkeys in a meat locker. The bruises are like the bandage; it's no good guessing. But this is how you tell a whore in Uptown.

Public pay phones are always in use. You overhear the most personal conversations. "Oh, yeah? Who's threatening who?" a thin white woman in hair curlers says into the receiver. Her face is defended by pencil-trimmed eyes. A toddler with its thumb in its mouth clings to her slacks. "Suck my box, that's what you can do."

On Argyle, where the A train stops—a main drag—a couple of men and a woman are warming their hands over a fire in a trash can; passing a bottle in a wrinkled brown bag. The strip-mined faces of Uptown; drought; soil erosion; acts of God. The store windows are soaped, as for Halloween; the sidewalks look scabby; the fire smokes and snaps. The woman is wearing sunglasses, earmuffs, a fur coat split up the back. "This neighborhood is really going to the dogs," she is saying —loudly, wanting people to hear. The undesirable elements, maybe? Who can they be? But all this means is that everyone is aware of degradation in Uptown. Everyone feels it. Everyone has the right to object.

"I'll drink to that," says one of her companions, tilting up his chin under the paper sack.

But Chicago winters are not all bad. We are a winter city, like Moscow; or, more to the point, Arkhangelsk, Vladivostok. Sometimes it gets cold, really cold; ten or fifteen below.

69

An icy vengeful exterminating cold, sweeping down from the north like a moral force. Dung freezes in the street; germs drop dead; vermin starve. It strikes at corruption. Breathing seems less injurious. The air is pure and full of truth. Walking down Sheridan, Argyle, on my way to the library, I was in a position to appreciate this.

If not for the medical dictionary, there would have been hardly any traffic to speak of at our reference desk. Borglum Branch was not very busy. A sort of club of elderly gentlemen competed daily for possession of *Barron's* and *The Wall Street Journal.* Miss Rose kept the papers in her right-hand drawer, which smelled of wrapped mints. She was forever melting mints on her tongue; it made her look mischievous, up to something. Friendly, the permissive type. (Mrs. Speer, the head librarian, was the other—the watchdog type. Censorship by steely-rimmed stare. Hence the lurid books in locked cases.) If Miss Rose kept the papers tucked away, it was just an excuse, a decoy; so she could lure these shy old birds into a little conversation. "How are *you* today, Mr. Adorno?" She knew them all by name. A grittily poor neighborhood—despairingly poor; the most desperate, down and out in all the city; a terminal case; but the financial pages were in brisk demand, and the old men trembled when they asked—eying the drawer.

"You don't have today's? Yesterday's will do."

Patrons—the regulars: the ones who showed up day after day and took the same places at the same tables—were familiar with our Rules. Knew them better than we did. Any violation they took almost personally. They were very strict in particular about observing Silence.

Something was the matter with the fan belt of the forced-air blower system. It made scandalized little noises. Tsk tsk tsk. The building itself was new: revolving glass doors, large plate windows—you could watch the icicles glibly dripping—but the reading room was the usual drowsy overheated affair: dim shelves, stacks of newsprint, tables of thick ugly honest oak and lampshades a suspicious green, like billiard cloth. And every time the heat went on it started clicking. The regulars objected to such distraction. This was supposed to be a library, wasn't it? People had a right to expect *quiet?* They knew their rights. Where else could they ever hope to enforce any.

But it was Miss Rose herself who was the heaviest offender.

I may as well get it over with—the whole description. The bright shy near-sighted gaze; the long cheeks puddled with rouge; the face dusted with powder like thick pink pollen. Miss Rose always seemed to be blushing. The glasses thumping on her nose, or—from a chain—on her flat sliding bosom. All this was loosely assembled. If she pushed in her blouse, her slip would peep out; if she hiked up her slip, a button would pop. Something had to give. You never could find a pencil when she was around. She stuck them all in her hair.

She hiked back and forth, lugging books—hugged to her chest, tucked under her chin—looking as if she was about to drop them. The only thing she never dropped was her voice. Even the regulars never got used to it.

Here was a new twist. The patrons telling the librarian to shut up.

"For shame, it's not ladylike," one gray-haired woman complained to me. "It's not *refined.* Who does she think she is? Anyhow? Acting like she owns the place."

Peevishly small; dainty; strings dangling from her plastic rainbonnet. Her gym shoes had no laces and her fur coat was fastened with diaper pins. " 'Her voice was ever soft, gentle and low,' " she quoted, laying a finger to her lips. "Pass it on to Miss Rose, why don't you?"

Miss Rose had her admirers too. Mr. Herman had been after her to go out with him for years. He was another of our regulars: tall, bald, high-shouldered, stiff-necked; rigidly polite. The back of his neck seemed very bare. His brows reached over the rims of his glasses. I think he had had a stroke at one time; the old man had a lip like a flat tire. It sagged when he smiled. He knew what hope was worth; a kite trapped in branches. Still he kept asking for *The Wall Street Journal.*

Miss Rose would hand it up, slyly sucking on her mint. But her voice reached all the way to the *Z*'s. "You see? I was saving it. Just for you."

Armchairs were provided, sunnier spots before the big dusty windows. But regulars had no use for these. Wouldn't be caught dead. Too casual, maybe. Their habits were more rigorous. They were not here for browsing; that had to be understood. For them the library was an alternative to idleness. Lean men from the queues at the day-labor agencies on Wilson Avenue; old ladies speedy in sneakers, in fur coats fallen on evil days. Pensioners poring over Moody's guides, Standard & Poor's, their hats at their sleeves. The fascination of the impoverished with the stock market reports seemed brutal to me, like the preoccupation of the diseased with the medical dictionary. Wouldn't they have been better off stuffing their shoes? But they were fans, like any others. For some it's sports, movie stars; for them it was the symbols of wealth and power. Age, failure, sickness, neglect; these were only temporary reversals. The utilities disconnected, the heat shut off. One could live with such interruptions. In the meantime, they dreamed of killings. The thin pages—*Barron's* airmail edition—rattled in their shaky hands. The reverence of old age.

Let us speak frankly. Where are people to go? People, I mean, who have no place to go. There are no clean well-lighted places. Bus stations are sorrowful, with all those black boxes that come to life if you drop in a quarter. The downtown movie houses which used to stay open all night—the ushers nudged you by the shoulder if you started snoring out loud —have changed over to porno flicks and charge too much money. I am thinking, of course, of the Clark Theater. The Clark was once the most illustrious of such institutions. It *was* an institution—a cultural crossroads. The Clark served Art too. The odors of winos' holey socks mingled powerfully with the dust of Desenex in college boys' sneakers. This is Chicago, you have to understand. We are not in the same line of business as Paris, London or New York. Though what our line of business is I'd dearly love to know.

What if it has something to do with places like the Clark.

It stayed open twenty hours out of the twenty-four. Tickets were cheap, the double bill changed daily. Another thing that changed very often was the seats. Patrons popped in and out of them with strange regularity. Watching *Grand Illusion, The Thirty-Nine Steps,* you couldn't help taking in all this restless activity out of the corner of your eye.

The seats squeak. Half of them are broken. Eyes slide—oily surfaces in the flickering light. Under folded jackets, in hidden laps, fingers are creeping. Hey. What's this? A hand on my thigh? Out of the dark your neighbor shoots a weasel-faced glance. Slowly, stealthily, with painful efforts at concealment —extra distracting—his zipper starts to creak. Just a little at a time. Same way the ladies in the balcony peel their candy bars.

The Ladies Gallery in the balcony is a special feature of the Clark. "For Ladies Only." This does not necessarily mean for the faint-hearted. Some come to make themselves at home; straddle their seats boldly. Two seats, three seats, a shopping bag on either side. Even their wigs sit sidewise. The shopping bags get noisier as they get emptier.

Sometimes it happens that a man turns up in the Ladies

Gallery—maybe he didn't notice the sign. A likely story. As far as the ladies are concerned, it's intentional. If looks could kill. All up and down the rows they are stabbing him with hatpins. Get a load of this guy. Sneaking down, trying to make himself look small; making off he just wants to watch the movie. Uh huh. We know what he wants. Take advantage of your tired, your poor, your huddled masses, will he? The lousy bum can't even *read*.

Someday the worm will turn, the meek will inherit the earth, the righteous will be justified. But not yet. Is nothing sacred? A man is occupying the Ladies Gallery.

Now what's wrong with this fellow next to you? He hasn't stopped squirming for a minute. All of a sudden he stiffens in his seat—you can feel it jerk. His heels grip, his head flies back. A few small defenseless whimpers; then a grunt, a very minor satisfaction. The seat sags, the tension goes. He jumps up right away, his jacket limp over his arm. No rest for the wicked. Off to look for another seat.

His place is taken at once—at sixty cents a head the Clark gets crowded—but this time it's a more familiar type. A classic. The Clark Street panhandler: an old-fashioned, inoffensive derelict—upturned collar, jaw sugared with whiskers. Clothes brown and dusty as leaves in a gutter. He loosens his shoelaces, stretches his legs. His chin starts to sink, his head nods to his chest. With a loud snickering snore it drops on your shoulder.

Saturday nights it was the motorcycle crowd, like divers in wetsuits in tight black leather. The sailors from Great Lakes, cheeks hidden in their collars. For all I know they're still there. Like the mirrors that seem to be blasted with buckshot; the toilets that keep running but never flush; the carpets that remind you of small animals flattened on a highway; no telling what they were once upon a time either. Though the management must have taken down the Fred Astaire posters. The Clark no longer serves the same mission.

On the last night before the change in policy, a brawl broke out. A drunk got rowdy, broke a bottle, started wielding its jagged neck. No one wanted to get near him. The audience whistled and stamped as if something had gone wrong with the sound track. At last a lanky shape detached itself from a seat on the aisle and pointed a gun. It was very dark, of course, hard to see. But all the movie *aficionados* recognized the weapon, the steely gleam. We weren't Humphrey Bogart fans for nothing.

"Hey, you. Yeah, you. You spoilin my view. I'se fixin to watch the movie."

It was an Orson Welles festival. *The Magnificent Ambersons.* Bustles, ostrich plumes, Joseph Cotten. The ushers arrived. The drunk left gladly. Other patrons followed him in droves —chased him through the lobby, swinging shopping bags and salvaged newspapers. They were the ones with the real beef. Just trying to get even. Who can afford three bucks? Who wants to watch dirty movies? Where would they go tomorrow?

At least the public libraries are still in business.

We had our flurries of activity.

On Friday afternoons, the barroom bets. On payday people get into aimless arguments. World records, batting averages; the age of the Pope; the name of President McKinley's assassin. This would mean a delegation; three, four heavy-set men, hot under the collar, elbowing and shoving. "This the reference?"

They fixed their eyes on the green blotter.

"We want to see a book. 'If,' a poem by Rudyard Kipling."

" 'If you can keep your wits when all about you—' "

"It's *head,* stupid."

"*Wits,* nit-wit. *Wits.*"

"And I say it's *head.*"

"It's *head,*" I said, looking up.

Wrong move.

They all glared down at me. Solid stares. What are you, a wise a guy or something? Who's asking you? Even the one who had his money on *head* was against me, his lip lifting at the corner, his face redder than the rest. I couldn't help thinking of the social-protest films of the thirties—the ones they used to run all the time at the Clark—the scene where the gang of striking workers with hats in their hands confronts the Big Boss, smoking and swiveling. Did I expect them to take my word for it, just because I was sitting behind a desk?

"Talk is cheap, sister. Can you show us in a book?"

That was the catch. I didn't know where to find anything. Couldn't make heads or tails of the reference desk. I was a library *intern*—maybe they called it *technician*. Something scientific anyway. I forget. To me what mattered was that you could work halftime. And with the public library—nothing if not literal—half really meant half. Eighteen and three-quarters hours, half the thirty-seven-and-one-half-hour week. Half the vacation pay, half the sick leave, half the insurance coverage. And so on. Anyone who has ever had a part-time job will know that this was not a bad deal. Once again, I was in a position to appreciate. I've had a lot of part-time jobs in my life.

One of our patrons was on to me. He came in regularly with a quotation for me to look up. "Let's see. What'll it be this time? I know—how about Thoreau? That business about the distant drummer. That oughta be real easy for you. I'll even give you a hint. The odds are on *Walden.*"

He was a big, red-faced, Sterno-breathed man in a peacoat and blond crew cut—picked rough rows sticking up—usually towing a little boy by the mitten strings. This kid was bundled

76

within an inch of his life—a papoose on a board. He could barely move his legs, they were so stuffed in boots and leggings, and his hood, pulled down and puckered over his eye, made him look mad at the world. His nose was always running.

"How about this here book?" the father would say, tapping the glass. Our reference books also stood guard behind glass. Stooping and squinting at some cracked gold-stamped binding. *"Beloved Hymns and Popular Verse.* Hmm. On second thought, that's not so hot. Tell you what—don't mess around. You want to make things easy for yourself, just look it up in *Bartlett's."*

A friendly warning from your local vigilante. Did they make the rounds, visit other branches too? As time went by, he gave up on the introductions. He'd just march up to the desk, stand stock still, square his shoulders, hook his thumbs in his belt loops.

" 'Shoot if you must this old gray head/But touch not your country's flag she said.' "

The little boy frowned at me and licked his clear shining lip.

But the one outstanding fact of life at Borglum Branch—the fact that so many of our patrons seemed to have nowhere else of any significance to go—was never mentioned. It was unmentionable. "She's very good with the old people," I heard Mrs. Speer saying into the phone. (A conversation about Miss Rose's everlasting promotion?) She meant the regulars. But she did not know that that was what she meant. Regulars weren't a category, weren't official. There was no way to count them, so they didn't count. Regulars didn't even have library cards. What for? Who needed cards? They practically lived in the library.

Popkin, a thin, scraggly, timid-looking soul, with a scrawny neck and a military overcoat that dragged to his ankles—

Russian Army issue—went tottering in and out of the stacks to a rapid shuffle. Toppling almost—pitched forward, on tiptoe—his eyes lifted in a startled expression. His white hair was thick as a cocoon and clamped in earmuffs, big black patches, that gave him the look of a horse in blinders. He always carried a book under his arm, pressed to his side. He was hatching it.

Miss Rose told me that he was a poet.

But what if you said, "But, Miss Rose, have you noticed? Popkin comes every day? All day? And night? In and out of the stacks—on tiptoe?" What would happen if you said this?

And what about Judge Brady? Not a real judge; he just looked like one. In the South they would have called him "Colonel." His profile plunged forward, his hair plowed back —stiff, erect, slick white goose feathers. His brow was polished and brown with freckles; his chin was doubled. The whole bust gave off a thick ruddy glow. Age had not diminished him; he loomed with it, powerfully, like a pile of rock.

It was a pleasure to watch him take his seat. First he unwound the long scarf from his neck, folded his coat, laid his hat on top of it over the back of the chair. He shook out his handkerchief, whisked it over the table, and laid his magnifying glass on top of that. He fished his watch out from under its flap and wound it with his thumb, consulting the clock on the wall. He put it back. He placed both hands on the table, lowered himself and scraped in his chair. At closing time the whole show ran backward. He pushed out his chair, raised himself up; two fingers digging his watch pocket—this wouldn't have been possible sitting down—looked at his watch, looked at the wall. Suddenly remembering another engagement. As if regulars ever left before closing time. Yes, what about him.

Or Mr. Adorno. At eighty, writing the story of his life. It was the story of his opinions, actually; he was against coeduca-

tion and in favor of the Kerensky government. A tidy little
man, a baked-apple face, eyes enlarged inside his glasses. His
teeth too; clamped like a vise. This gave him a fierce look
when he came up to the desk and asked me to read back to
him what he had written. "To make sure it's eligible." He
used ruled notebooks, but his handwriting was too big to stay
on the lines. And I think he just liked to agree with himself;
listening, lost in admiration, his eyes lurking, motionless, in
their depths. "Yes, yes. That's right. Right absolutely." His
starched collar looked sharp enough to slash his throat. His
fountain pen leaked—there was a spreading blue blot on his
nice white shirtfront. "That hits the nail right on the head."

Of course, there were cranks. For instance, a tall straight old
woman, dressed in gray from head to foot, like a Quaker or
Civil War nurse, with a strange flat yellow face, with feet laced
up in combat boots . . . she had been sighted all over the city;
a familiar figure at downtown hotels during conventions. She
just dropped in to use the plumbing. The toilet flushing con-
tinuously. It went on without letup. What could she be up to
in there? Who was about to go in and look? You just had to
wait until she decided to emerge, dripping wet, long, stringy,
gray as a mop, slapping the key on the counter and sloshing
out the door. Her boots tracking squishing puddles. It was the
dead of winter.

This, I admit, roused a few eyebrows; glances were exchanged, wild surmise. But that was all. Our business was
books; checking them in, stamping them out. Cataloguing.
Shelving. Minding our own business. At Borglum the level of
tolerance for individual extremes was very high. It had to be
—the facts were too peculiar. You couldn't let on, let the cat
out of the bag. That would have meant acknowledging . . . all
this other business. And that was the one thing that couldn't
be tolerated. To have characterized the services of the public
library in this way.

And what of the board of directors meetings downtown, at the main branch, the limestone white elephant on Michigan Boulevard? Guards, uniforms, badges posted everywhere; at the turnstile entrances, outside the public lavatories, on marble staircases with high carved mottoes. MCMXL . . . PRO BONO PVBLICO. . . Funny things go on in libraries; everyone knows that. It's got something to do with all those stacks; shelves and shelves of weighty books. Reason is a passion; an instinct, a drive. It's not so strange if citizens respond in its temples with primitive gestures; flashing switch-blades, unzipping flies. Plans were being drawn for the expansion and remodeling of the old building—its crossed swords, draped flags, shimmering flocks of pigeons. It couldn't be torn down; it could only be surrounded.

Did anyone ever get up at these meetings and say: "Fountains, shmountains. Do you think the bums from Clark Street will go for this? After all, they're the ones who spend the most time here. And what about the little old ladies with the shopping bags? If we make the joint look like Marshall Field's or Saks Fifth Avenue, will they feel at home?"

There were two schools of philosophy in the public library. One was that it existed for the sake of circulating books. The other was that it existed for the sake of preserving them. This is what it all boils down to, eventually, with any bureaucracy in the public service. Mrs. Speer belonged to the Public Enemy school.

She was nearing retirement—with some relief. Harried gray braids, wisps escaping; pale eyes fused to glass. She wore tailored suits and frilly blouses and the ruffles rode and swelled at her throat. She had no chin; when her upper lip snapped down, she looked like a turtle. Even patrons trying to return books were challenged at Borglum. They had to show identification. "Just in case." In case what? "You never know." Mrs.

Speer was proud of this rule—the only one like it in the city —but she knew I hated to ask; so she kept a sharp eye out whenever I worked behind the circulation desk. And as soon as she saw someone bursting through the doors with an armload of books, she'd come rushing out of her office, giving the ends of her jacket a smart yank with her knuckles.

"Don't you *dare* go letting them give any books back till they show who they are."

Borglum was losing customers steadily—but not so fast as it was losing books. Pasted above the check-out machine— where we could refer to it while stuffing pockets and stamping cards—was a list of delinquents: big-time offenders who owed hundreds of dollars in overdue fines and a.w.o.l. volumes. Names like Rockett J. Squirrell, J. Edgar Hoover, Hedy Lamarr. Books came back with bindings loose, pages ripped out, pictures defaced—mustaches, pubic hair, scratched in ballpoint pen. Some seemed to have been on a bender: dropped in hot bathtubs, propping windows. Greasy thumbprints, shopping reminders, telephone numbers, comments in the margins: "Bull." "That's what you think." "Proof?" "How true." These were the ones we got back—if we were lucky. The Public Enemy theory has its points.

Mrs. Speer's efficacy as a supervisor may have been rated in terms of circulation. But in her own heart she knew that her job—her sacred trust—was to protect the public from itself. There is a certain socialized insanity. (Once we start calling people cranks, where will we draw the line?) Schoolteachers used to be a prime example—I don't know if they are still. I recall a note pinned to the bulletin board in my high school principal's office—from a teacher who had retired to a chicken farm. I had been in her English class. We read *Ivanhoe*. That is, she read it—aloud—to us; sitting behind her desk, her cheek in her hand. A flowered smock, a crimped blue head. On her desk, under her desk, piled on window sills, radiators,

81

and from head to foot when she opened her closet, were stacks of colored notebooks. Theme papers. They were all on *Ivanhoe.*

You didn't get a grade if you didn't hand in a notebook. But everyone knew how grades were distributed in Miss Bozzich's class. Neat girls got E, girls who wore lipstick and blue jeans G. Short boys rated F. And boys who were tall, who had already outgrown the childish seats, whose long legs sprawled arrogantly in the aisle—i.e., bad boys—failed. Period. There was no appeal.

Each day, before Miss Bozzich began to read, someone had to get up in class and tell "the story thus far." As we progressed with the novel, these daily summaries naturally got longer. Besides, we were catching on; some of us could be long-winded. By the time we had finished with "the story thus far," and just about when Miss Bozzich—licking her fingertip, making a little light breeze of the pages—had found her place, the bell would ring. The nasty buzzer. Tin lockers slammed in the corridors. The heathen were on the march. We had reached an impasse. I remember the small stingy print, the crumbly paper—it broke off like soda crackers—pennants, visors, dark Rebecca. But we never got past page 99. Next semester it would begin all over again. English 1 2 3 4 5 6 7 8. No one ever finished *Ivanhoe.*

"My little chickadees are so nice and polite—so well behaved—so much more grateful than my *thankless pupils* ever were," poor Miss Bozzich had written.

Mrs. Speer already had her chickens.

These were the new books, stacked on a table in the back room in tall neat rows. On top of each pile a note: "Do Not Disturb, J. Speer." Mrs. Speer was cataloguing these books, and whenever she got the chance she would shut herself up with them. Books on the shelves were marked-down merchandise—spoiled, soiled, grubby, touched by too many hands.

Here they confronted her in their original splendor. New books don't smell as good as they used to—it must be the glue —but the bindings were still stiff and the pages fresh. Each and every one that came into Borglum Branch headed straight for the back. And it stayed there. When the table couldn't hold any more, stacks sprouted under the legs; then on filing cabinets, chairs. You didn't dare to move them. They were like that For A Reason. If things ever got mixed up, Mrs. Speer would have to Start All Over Again.

The thing was, the cataloguing had already been done—at the downtown library. The books came carded, pocketed and numbered, and all that was left were a few clerical tasks. Once upon a time cataloguing had been the special responsibility of the head librarian. Now there had been a reorganization; the librarians had been freed from their musty cubbyholes, ordered—in other words—into circulation. The job had switched from archives to public relations. That was the idea —not Mrs. Speer's idea at all. She had put up with it at first. Then her husband died. It was a bad time for her. She resumed cataloguing.

But there was too much for her to do; she couldn't make up her mind; she had lost the knack for decisions. Should it be 813? 973? You see? She talked about her "problems," the "tough nuts" she had "to crack." (Mrs. Speer loved slang; she was always pouncing on Miss Rose with a conniving sort of wink: "It's snowing below!"—Your slip is showing.) This was the secret of her mistreated glance and raveled braids.

It was the reason I had been hired; Mrs. Speer thought she wanted an assistant. She took me into her confidence—into the back room—and showed me the books mounting up, each separate pile with its own separate note. Weeks went by; no instructions. She put me to work typing file cards for volumes long retired from the shelves—"for practice." Then I arranged and rearranged stacks of yellow-bordered *National*

Geographics. Once I came upon her, humming, floating a pink feather duster over the books. Up went her ruffles; down went her lip. She hid the duster behind her back. She wasn't ready to relinquish her task—that is to say, the books.

Maybe she was protecting them in this way. Why catalogue? Why file? Why put books on the shelves? Why send them off to meet their fate—abandon them to the inevitable? Why start the whole damned thing all over again? She was weary of it all, the endless cycle, dreariness, decline, destruction. As I say, she had spent too much time in public facilities.

What with one thing and another, it was proving difficult to find a place for me at Borglum Branch. Regular employees were civil service; they had been fingerprinted at City Hall. They already had their places, their allotted tasks, and did not wish to share them. Beebee, perched on her high stool at the circulation desk, hunched over in characteristic bad posture, was not less protective of her overdue notices than Mrs. Speer was of her new books. Beebee was a bookworm, always hiding some contraband in her lap—Staff was not permitted to *read,* one of Mrs. Speer's phobias—and that was why she was always hunched over like that; glancing down possessively while her white fingers rippled the files. She was a lip-reader; the avid movements gave her away. A striking disorderly head; a thrusting nose; heavy Sephardic eyes. Her hair was coarse, crinkly and black as the wire pins that—more or less—skewered her bun. The bony ridges poked up on the back of her neck. The rich pink gums glowed when she smiled.

Beebee had a star-crossed love; her boyfriend, Henry, was not Jewish. It was supposed to be a secret. He met her at the branch—came to stand and gaze, leaning across the counter; her lips moving busily the while, her black head ducking over the files. He was tall, thin, in gym shoes and foggy glasses, and for a young man he was quickly losing his hair. After they said hello, that was it. They never seemed to need another word. From time to time, heaving a sigh, sinking her elbows onto her lap, Beebee would raise heavy eyes and gaze back.

Their romance was our current event; what we talked about over breaks in the kitchen while the teakettle whistled and the brown bags crackled. Should Beebee leave home and marry Henry? Defy her parents? Deny her faith? What if Henry converted? He looked convertible. Etc., etc. Beebee loved being the center of attention. Listening to advice, sipping sweet tea, her glance grew high-crested and dreamy. Still, she was a private and secretive soul. Most of us kept our lunches in the refrigerator, but Beebee stowed hers in her locker—bananas and all—her head poking behind the tin door as sharply, jealously, as it darted over her files. Fines, overdue notices, all that privileged information. You'd think she had something hidden in there. Books. The worst thing you can hide—in a library.

The clandestine had a natural appeal for Beebee. But Miss Rose took an anguished interest in her story; Miss Rose had a story of her own. At college she had been engaged to a medical student. Drafted as a medic, he was killed in the war. And after Stanley was killed . . .

"Well, after Stanley was killed, I knew I'd never find another man as good. 'What's the matter with you, Dora?' my mother would say. 'Why do you have to be so *choosy?* Do you want to end up with nothing? Is that what you want? Isn't any man in the world good enough for you?' Well, that wasn't it, but I just couldn't help it. She wouldn't understand. Not after Stanley."

She held her cup in both hands, her elbows planted on the table, steeped in bracelets; these bangles had a way of sliding up her thin arms. Her light eyes, flush with the level of steaming tea, filled and dimmed with reminiscences. When Miss Rose took off her glasses, her face was defenseless altogether. After Stanley.

I used to urge Miss Rose to take Mr. Herman up on his offer. People were always urging Miss Rose. "Why not go out with him? He looks presentable. He seems to be a gentleman."

"Oh, he is, he is." Miss Rose would hasten to defend him; after all, he was a suitor. "He is a gentleman. A gentleman of the old school. A gentleman and a scholar. You don't know Mr. Herman like I do."

"So? How come? What's the big deal?"

It seemed that she liked to be teased in this way. She didn't mind it, on a cold night, waiting at her bus stop. The spaces were wide and dark between the arc lamps and she was afraid to stand alone. Safe to talk when your bus was coming.

Who didn't urge Miss Rose? If she took a certain exam and passed it, she could become a head librarian herself with a branch of her own, and her salary would jump considerably. Everyone wanted her to do it. But Miss Rose was afraid to take this exam; she shuddered at the thought of it. The very mention sent her fluttering. And it must have been mentioned with some regularity; it had been going on for years. Like Mr. Herman.

"I don't know, I don't know," she said, glancing up the street. The lights of the bus coming to the rescue, sweeping snow before it, threshing it like wheat. She peeled off her glove to get at her change. She carried the exact fare in her mitt. "After all. After Stanley."

"Oh, Miss Rose. Don't give me that. You know yourself it's all a lot of baloney."

She put her head to one side in her fluffy angora hat, with its jingling sequin chains. Her tongue tasted her mint. "Yes," she said. "Yes, I know it." And climbed aboard in her galoshes.

What hope was there for Mr. Herman—keeping an eye on IBM, Bunker Ramo and Xerox, but stuffing his money in a mattress, a shoe, the lining of his coat? It looked lumpy. What chance did he have against a dead man, a war hero, and a doctor on top of it? How disappointed he looked whenever he found me sitting at her post. Lifting his eyebrows and laying his hat against his chest:

"No Miss Rose tonight?"

It was not that Miss Rose needed or wanted my assistance any more than anyone else; but she was softer than anyone else. She gave in. That was how I ended up passing most of my eighteen and three-quarters hours at the reference desk— the one place in that moribund facility where there really was the least to do. This was the backwater of backwaters. The fan belts clicked, icicles dripped; Judge Brady focused the light in his curved reading glass.

It was Miss Rose's responsibility to lock up most late nights, and it worried her to death. She was no authoritarian; not a bossy bone in her body. But some people don't like to be waked from their sleep. There were always patrons who objected. "Whaddaya mean, closing time? It's only five to nine." We closed at nine. When Alphonse, the pageboy, came rolling and rumbling his cart through the reading room, dumping books, clicking and dimming lights, it was taken as a personal insult. Regulars had squatters' rights.

There was one gaunt heavy-shouldered man who used to sit in the same position by the hour, his fingers bunched up, scooping his eyes. He came with a companion—another familiar type of the neighborhood: a mass of raw bones, dry hair, haggard fur. But she had been a beauty, had squandered great gifts; there was still a haughty distinction in her style. Her coat thrown open, her chair thrust back, her shins bare. When the time came she would reach out and shake him by the shoulder. Not everyone could be persuaded so gently. Shaken by the shoulder, they might not take it so well. Their sunken heads would lift with a growl. Their souls, off wandering, had not made it back.

Miss Rose could rise to the occasion.

"If you don't go quietly," she would say, her voice quavering and her eyes glittering a little above her rouge, "then— well, then—we'll just have to get the pageboy here to throw you out."

Alphonse's dark eyes lustrously widened. He was a high school student, a tall black youth—very tall; stooping; dawdling, dreamy; shooting up so suddenly to such a height seemed to have exhausted his energies—who kept to himself and had no inclination for being drawn out, either. He looked for cover behind his cart. At such times we were reminded of our lack of manpower. Another fact of life in a branch.

Beebee had been followed to her el station by one of our patrons. We all knew who this was. A slight young man— probably older than he looked—in leather jacket and blue jeans, with a high white forehead and rough blond hair. The kinky ridges clinging, clenched tight. He sat at the table, a pile of notebooks open before him, fists shoved into his pockets— shooting out cunning sidelong glances. He had a tic of some sort, a muscle jumping in his jaw. It made him look as if he might be grinning, but you couldn't tell for sure—he kept it up all the time. One foot never stopped tapping under the table; one patched knee jerked constantly up and down.

As soon as Beebee saw him, she scrambled off the stool and hid herself behind the high hedge of the circulation desk. He looked her way, grinning. He slid his fountain pen from inside his jacket, crouched over as if to write; thought better of it;

hid the pen again. Someone might be eavesdropping on him
—stealing his thoughts—tuning in on his secrets. The world
was watching him, wondering about him, trying to guess; he
had to be careful, clever and sly.

It was a dreary night, fit only for regulars. Darkness
crowded the windows, Alphonse's cart rolled over the boards.
Judge Brady, at the same table, was peering through his magnifying glass, his head reared back, his lips clasped in satisfaction. Someone snored under the green lampshade, a cheek on
an arm. As for the gray-haired woman with the agile eyes and
the diaper pins, it was Miss Rose as usual she was watching.
What could that loud—that brazen—creature be up to now?

Miss Rose strode up, heels rapidly battering, her glasses on
their chain pounding against her chest. No sooner had she
leaned down to the young man—his head, half hidden,
seemed to be crouching behind his shoulder—than he was up
with a bound. His chair crashed backward. His fist struck the
table.

"Goddam all you lousy Jews. Always telling people what to
do. I'm not taking any orders from you."

"Please lower your voice," Miss Rose said thickly, her heart
at once in her throat. "Please remember. This is a library."

"Don't have to fuckin tell me what it fuckin is. Full of fuckin
niggers and Jews. That's all you got. Think you're running the
whole goddam show."

There was a murmur throughout the room. The financial
pages stopped rustling. "Such langwidge," the old lady whispered, clicking her tongue. Then all you could hear were the
fan belts clicking. Tsk tsk tsk.

"If you feel that way—if that's the way you feel . . ." Miss
Rose fingered her chain. The artificial color stood out in her
cheeks. "If you're not going to keep your voice down . . ."
But no one was listening. She wasn't listening herself. He had
all the attention now. And he knew it. Glancing round craftily,

89

his jaw clenching and grinning, taking it all in. All the shocked wrinkled faces, the Woolworth's specs pressing their cheeks like paperweights.

"Don't have to fuckin tell me to fuckin leave," he said, piling up his books with a thump. "I'm leaving, all right. I'm leaving. But I'll be back." He zipped his jacket to his chin and tossed his head. "I'll be back. And when I come you better look out. You better get ready for me, I'm warning you. Because I'm going to fix all you lousy creeps if it's the last thing I do."

"Oh, yeah?"

This was Mr. Herman, rising, drawing up his shoulders. "Why don't you start right now, then?" He slammed his hat on the skin of his head.

"Oh, yeah?"

Mr. Adorno. He kicked out his chair. His glasses had a dark sparkle. All over the room chairs were scraping. Pensioners rising; sleepers waking. The boy threw his books down and put up his fists. His elbows in leather sleeves gripped his chest. The old men too put up their fists, began moving in, waving their arms. They danced up and back and pumped up and down. Old-fashioned boxers with old-fashioned rules. Judge Brady stood firm, one foot planted forward, one arm doubled up in front of the other, his chin to his chest. His back was most honorably arched.

Miss Rose tugged Mr. Herman's sleeve. He shook her off. "He started it." The back of the old man's neck stood stiff. They were waiting for the other to swing first. He did. His arm shot out, snapped back; his jaw gave a twitch. The old woman gasped; this was for real.

Mr. Herman took his swing. His arm stuck out like a bat; it swung him halfway about. He missed by a mile. The boy rocked back and forth, his head dodging and ducking behind his raised knuckles.

"C'mon, c'mon. What's the matter? Chicken? I thought you wanted a fight. Hey, you old boys. You old bums. C'mon. How about it? What are you waiting for? Six against one. You're all a bunch of crazies, you know that? Misfits. That's all you got."

The situation was getting serious. I mean sensitive. It wasn't so much that we were afraid he was going to land a punch and hurt anyone—though his knuckles looked sharp, they could mark an old face. But what if one of the boxers should have a heart attack and drop right on the spot? That was the danger. All this dancing, hard breathing, crowding the enemy. Such excitement was too much for them. But who was going to say it? There are injuries and injuries. They were sick and tired too; sick and tired of being old, weak, damaged, done for, counted out. They weren't taking any more. They had had enough. The worm was turning, the meek were inheriting the earth. It wasn't the time to call attention to the facts.

"Isn't this the *limit?*"

The little old lady clasped her hands to her chin. She was in seventh heaven. Mr. Adorno was hopping up and down, thumbing his nose and baring his big teeth. Popkin was tiptoeing round and round, hugging his book tenderly under his arm. A punch landed. Oof. Whose? Where? They had him surrounded, they were closing in. A stringy arm hooked him by the collar, another by the belt. "That's right, boys," Judge Brady shouted. "The back of the neck and the seat of the pants."

"I'll get even—I'll get even." His heels were kicking; they had pinned his sleeves to his sides.

"Let's show him the door, boys."

They hoisted him up and hustled him out. All you could see was a head hanging forward, the shoulders of the leather jacket lifted like football pads. "Kikes. Crazies. Niggers. Bums. Look at you. All of you. They oughta lock you all up."

Pretty soon the police arrived, a low-slung pair in fur-collared jackets. They stood dripping and wiping their caps. It had started to snow and heavy clots were sliding off and melting all around them.

They settled their caps on their heads. "Now. What's this all about? What seems to be the trouble?"

It was past nine, but none of the regulars had left and no one expected them to. Now everyone started talking at once. Everyone seemed to have a complaint to make, an insult, an injury. They had been saving it up. Now was the chance. The old woman fastened the strings of her rain bonnet under her chin. What was the world coming to? You heard everything these days. Why just the other— Miss Rose, under compulsion, was forcing herself to repeat the threatening words. Beebee, still ducking behind the desk, was telling of the times she had been followed. Mr. Adorno had heard noises under his window. Someone had seen a knife. The cops, listening to all this, were more and more and more unmoved. They didn't exactly look at anybody. Their eyes grazed over the faces. The weak, the outraged, the indignant. *Big* deal. Hey, grandpa. Isn't it about time you were home in bed? Now and then they glanced at one another; you could see what they were thinking. Kikes. Crazies. Niggers. Bums.

They held up their hands. "Okay, okay. Cool it. Everyone. Pipe down. Now. One at a time. Let's have it again."

"And here's Judge Brady. And he'll tell you. He saw the knife."

"Judge?" said the cop, "Is he really a judge?" For the first time lifting his eyes and looking round with a flicker of interest. Judge Brady had posted himself outside to keep watch. He came in to report. His scarf was dragging, his galoshes unbuckled; he was hoarse with excitement and blowing his nose on his sleeve. His face was the color of a bowl of borscht.

92

"Snowing so hard you can't tell much," he trumpeted, and dashed out again.

The cop looked sleepy. He went to the desk and asked Beebee for the key; he wanted to use the bathroom. "Give us another call if this guy shows up again," the other said, taking a look around; a last browsing glance. Some dump. For the second time that night, the unmentionable had almost been mentioned.

The officers left and we locked up. Came a pounding at the door, a face pressed to the glass. It was only Henry, calling for Beebee. He had come to take her to her el stop. Patrons, staff, made the rounds together; peeping in lockers, round doors, testing latches, switching lights. In the back room Mrs. Speer's books towered undisturbed. Ziggurats. When Miss Rose had locked the front doors, she turned around and locked them again, her fingers fumbling with the keys. Then she flung the keys down the mouth of the book depository. She never carried them off with her. What if she took that exam and passed it? That's what she was afraid of. Bad enough to have to lock up on dark nights.

It was snowing forcefully by now; not one of your fresh swirling fleecy snows. It wasn't going to be a white Christmas. This was a wet cutting sleet and the wind off the lake was blowing it all sideways. It seemed yellow in the lamplight, the sidewalks soaked. All those bare legs, gym shoes, cracked soles, creaking in the mush. It grappled with coat collars, clutched at necks. The streetlights were melting. Judge Brady and Mr. Adorno appointed themselves to escort the old lady. Others trudged off, looking back over their shoulders; remembering the late hour and the grimness of the neighborhood. As if such general misery were not a safe-conduct.

Mr. Herman—trying to touch his hat brim in the slashing

sleet—offered his elbow and asked Miss Rose if he might see her home. She demurred. Of course. She would always demur. But after all, tonight was different. It was time for a little charity. She consented to be walked as far as her bus stop. Her tinsel was shivering. He grasped her arm, she pinched his thick sleeve, and they bowed their heads to the snow.

TWENTY-SIXTH AND CALIFORNIA

It is almost impossible to make out what is actually going on in a criminal courtroom, but you can tell at a glance, through the crack in the doors, what stage has been reached. If the benches are packed; if the air is thick; if people are moving all the time, going in and out—the heavy doors constantly creaking—then it is only the beginning. A bond hearing, maybe; prisoners being hauled in fresh from the lockup.

All the old-fashioned courtrooms look alike. The raised bench, the striped flag behind the chair. The clerk's desk with its green lampshade and batteries of rubber stamps. Manacles gleaming on the bailiff's hip. Calendar pages pasted on the wall. No Smoking signs. (You could cut it with a knife.) Flypaper shades—long tattered strips—buckling at the windows. The glass glitters between with intense prairie light. The big rotating fans are not stirring now, but you can imagine what it must be like in summer.

The name is called; the charge is muttered; a shuffle along the crowded rows—relatives, friends, rising to come forward and stand behind the accused. Court is above all a family affair. The benches are full of children, like eighteenth-century jails.

"This is Willie Monroe's mother, Your Honor. She has nine other children at home and she's on public aid. If the bond isn't lowered, she won't be able to raise the money to get him out."

To get out—that's the object. Everyone knows it; it's no secret here.

The judges also look alike, with their bent heads, bald spots, shoulders in black judicial robes. "If I set bond at three thousand dollars, you have to come up with ten percent. That means three hundred dollars. Think you can raise three hundred over the telephone?"

Thud, thud, the clerk stamps the papers. The turnover is rapid, more or less automatic; it seems to be the court's main

96

business too. Meanwhile they're singing harmony in the lockup. Every time the clerk opens the door and sticks his head inside—calling a name into its barred depths—you can hear the notes escaping to a stomping rhythm.

"Hey. See that? See that there?" A bunch of little boys, growling whispers. Pointing across the fire escape at the grim bricked wall of the county jail. "That where you gonna end up, LeRoy." Holding their stomachs with laughter. "Hey, LeRoy. LeRoy. Your granddaddy gonna git hisself locked up with you?"

The big flinty block at Twenty-sixth and California really does seem to stand in the midst of a prairie, open to the elements. The windows look far out over the vast industrial plain of Chicago. It shimmers with power; the mighty haze hurts your eyes. On the slopes along the front steps—the name, CRIMINAL COURTS, set in a mound—signs warn you: KEEP OFF THE GRASS. Though the grass looks tough enough to fend for itself. So do the matrons who frisk you when you enter. On the women's side, they do a land-office business in Mace. The small black spray dispensers are dumped out of purses by the dozens. An old black man, bald as a crab apple, briskly snaps a rag at the shoeshine stand, an official seated before him, one foot mounted on the stirrup, briefcase across his lap. I don't know, maybe it wasn't such a hot idea to build a city on this site. There is too much energy here. Along with the power of construction goes a power of destruction. Tohu and bohu. Vacant lots, buildings condemned, neighborhoods decayed. Chicago isn't a city: just the raw materials for a city. The prairie is always reasserting itself, pressing its claims.

At preliminary hearings in Felony Court the benches are crowded with plaintiffs.

A young black woman in aviator glasses, a natural, a raincoat over her arm; flanked before the bar by two state's attor-

97

neys. On the other side stands a bushy-haired black youth, his red shirttail hanging out. Who is his counsel?

The clerk raises a rasping voice.

"Pub-lic de-fen-der? Pub-lic de-fen-der?"

A slim smooth-haired fellow in a light suit strolls up the aisle, head elevated, chewing gum.

"This yours?" the clerk says from the height of his desk, pointing down at the head of the accused. Who glances sluggishly over his shoulder, a gaze dull in dark glasses. It's as if you'd stirred mud.

"Please state your name and spell it. . . . Where were you at eight fifty-five on the night of . . ." They have to caution the plaintiff to speak up. She raises her chin firmly, but her voice is still low.

A washroom on a college campus. She heard footsteps, someone entering, but she was washing her hands over the sink and didn't look up. When she turned to reach for a paper towel, shaking her hands, she came face to face with the defendant. He was standing at arm's length, a knife stretched between them. He told her not to scream, to keep quiet, to shut up. He backed her into a toilet stall.

"And what happened then?"

No one pays attention at hearings. It's too hard. Witnesses' backs are turned, you can't make out what's being said. People keep coming and going, infants smacking their pacifiers. Children stretched out fast asleep, the mark of the hard bench on their cheeks. Besides—no one has come to listen. They all have troubles of their own. Every time the door gives a scrape, all the heads go up—row after row. But by now the whole room has sensed what's up; everyone knows "what happened then." You can even hear the plunging keys of the stenotype machine.

The public defender's eyes are black and bright in their cavities. "What time was your class over on the night of

. . . And you were still in the building? At eight-fifty-five?
. . ." His voice skeptically rising. "Speak up, speak up. The
court stenographer can't record you nodding your head." He
seems to move toward her, to crowd her. It's as if he too is
backing her up, bullying, closing in; his chin thrust forward,
rapidly snapping his gum. She clasps her coat in front of her.
He probes the details, over and over. *Toilet toilet toilet.* Every
time he says it, people smile, cast glances over their shoulders.
Comments are passing from ear to ear.

The defendant stands unmoved, neck forward, hands
loosely clasped behind his back. He has said nothing; nodded
only once, in response to his name.

Roughly speaking, there are only two kinds of people in a
criminal courtroom. Innocent, guilty, have nothing to do with
it. Plaintiffs and defendants are not on different sides; they are
not opposing forces. They belong to the same category, are
drawn from the same human mass. Almost everyone on the
benches is black. And—although there are a lot of dragging
fur-trimmed coattails, broad-brimmed hats, platform heels
striking loudly in the corridors—they are, even more over-
whelmingly, the bleak, unstylish poor. Drab winter coats cling
like burdens to their backs. Children especially are buttoned
to the eyes, such stiffened little bundles they can scarcely move
their limbs. Maybe that's why they're so good. They are bored
and frightened and fall asleep from stupefaction. Glancing
about these crowded rows, men with hats on their knees,
women rocking babies on their laps, one fact strikes you—you
can't tell who is who, what they are here for. There is no
special face of injury, no protest. No one seems to have any
axes to grind. Nothing seems to separate outlaws from their
victims.

In the other category—on the other side of the great divide
—are the officials. The professional, administrative class.

White men in business suits with important documents under their arms. That is where the lines are drawn. It is the only line. For everyone else, the impression is of a sort of soup kitchen; something being ladled, doled out—made to go around. The law is a tedious, passionless process, and they have fallen into its hands.

In Violence Court—murder inquests—something unusual: a fussing infant. The mother and grandmother are trying to keep it quiet. Mexican women, in mourning; their faces bend over the child and black lace drapes their cheeks. The matron, with her burly white sleeves, her vest and bailiff's star, her great festooned wig like a silken lampshade, leans over the back of the bench to caution them. They pass the baby back and forth, thumping its back. There are circles of gold in its little dark ears.

A detective from Homicide is called to the stand, and a man rises from the back row, cap in hand, to go up and sit at the long table. He is wretchedly dressed: dilapidated shoes, scuffed rubbers, a torn T-shirt stretched over a flabby belly, a matted jacket crushed under his arm. Small bloodshot bewildered eyes.

The detective had been called to the flat of Marvella Washington, late wife of Freddie Washington, and found a dead woman lying across the bed, sheets soaked with blood. She had been stabbed in the throat and shot in the stomach. The detective called upon her estranged husband; he denied any knowledge of his wife's murder and agreed to take a lie detector test. A couple of days later, the detective picked up Freddie Washington and asked him to come to the station for the polygraph. Freddie Washington changed his story. He said his wife had called him and asked him to come over to discuss child support. He told her he would but fell asleep instead and when he woke it was 2 A.M. He hailed a cab and went to her

100

apartment. She buzzed him in. When he got upstairs, she went into the bedroom. He followed. She made straight for the bed, reached under the pillow, and when she turned to face him she was holding a knife in one hand and a revolver in the other. She brandished the weapons. He grabbed her wrists. She fell across the bed and he heard the gun go off. He turned her over. The knife was sticking out of her throat. The children were still asleep in the other room. He took the gun, wiped the knife, and went downstairs to get another cab. In the back seat he hid the weapons, shoved them down between the arm and the cushion. He got out at his apartment and went upstairs to bed.

The baby keeps crying the whole time, sucking and squeezing on an empty bottle. It sounds sick. Freddie Washington's counsel moves for dismissal on grounds that no crime has been committed. The charge will be involuntary manslaughter. Chairs thud at the table. Freddie Washington rises indecisively, fingers gripping his cap. What happens next? His brow is blunt, stunned, right between the eyes. So that's the meaning of their glazed pink expression. A steer slamming down the ramp at the stockyards. His attorney takes hold of him by both shoulders and turns him about, pointing him in the proper direction.

A woman sitting across the aisle nudges her companion. Time to go. The women rise and start shaking, waking, various children—heads popping up all over the place, staring round with shocked marvelous eyes. I remember all at once that I have been a child napping on these benches myself. There might be eight or ten of them, and they all seem the same age. The mothers scold them. Have they got everything? Boots? Mittens? They come wading up the aisle in unbuckled galoshes, half awake, the women dragging two, three limp arms by each hand. They must have had something to do with the case; but you would never have guessed that was what they were here for. The two women had listened to the entire proceedings unmoved. Relatives? Whose? Were they with Freddie Washington or against him? And what about the children? Were some of them the couple's orphans?

The detective admitted that no effort had been made to locate the taxi Freddie Washington took home. You can't exactly blame him. They are mostly gypsy cabs, without radios, without licenses. Finding one that had traversed the ghetto at three in the morning would be like looking for a phantom ship in a phantom ocean. The address was on Sixty-third Street. Woodlawn: the neighborhood is shell-shocked, ravaged by slum fires. Abandoned buildings, jagged windows, blackened girders of the el tracks. Talk about the power of darkness. Children hunt cockroaches trickling through the rubble—spray them with Flit cans. ("I got 'm. I got 'm. Look how he curl up all his skinny little legs.") The elevated went up in 1893 to trundle ladies in bustles and whalebone to the world's fair. Now it comes pitching round the bend, shooting out sparks, eyeball to eyeball with smashed glass, bombed-out craters, curtains fluttering like torn stockings. At Stony Island, the terminus, it sits and shudders for a while. Nothing around but the prairie.

The further along the legal process, the emptier the courtroom. That's axiomatic. The benches shine like church pews. There are fewer cases on the dockets—but that's not the real reason. It's those calendar pages on the wall. Too much time has passed.

The bailiff is taking a siesta in the jury box, tilted back in the swivel chair with his feet up on the rail: a huge black man, powerful rolls of fat, his white shirtfront spread like a tablecloth, a feast. The clerk's green sleeves move under the desk lamp. The hands click on the clock face. A hat lies atop a folded overcoat in a corner of a bench; a shopping bag from Treasure Island is shoved under a seat. Could be someone's lunch.

This is a murder trial in its seventh week. Court was scheduled to reconvene at one-thirty. At that time the jury, coming from lunch, emerged in a body from their special elevator—gates clanking in the silence of the corridor—and were herded into the jury room in back. A large diagram leans against an easel, the ground plan of the first floor of a house in the 5200 block of South Green Street.

All the houses on that block happen to be alike: solid yellow-brick lozenges; stone-step side entrances, fenced symmetrical front lawns. Grass grows in cracks in the sidewalks and small saints in grottoes stand in the yards. The neighborhood is just south of the now defunct stockyards, where, once upon a time, most of the residents earned their livings. Like Mayor Daley's neighborhood, a couple of miles to the north along Halsted Street. Mayor Daley was a blue-collar mayor in a blue-collar town and that was his strength. ("Chicago *works!*") He got his power straight from the source: smokestacks, boxcars, steam whistles, steel mills. You call a wrong number and get the bridge over the Cal Sag Canal. Choked waters, chugging tankers, smudged air, slag heaps. World without end. The bridge-tender, friendly, is munching a sandwich. "Meat loaf and mustard," he explains over the telephone. The mayor was one of us.

But his personal protection did not extend to this block on Green Street. A few years back, black families began moving in from the south and east. Pressures were building. The summer passed without any special incident here though there was continuous rioting in Calumet Park—whites running down the beach, stoning blacks sitting on their blankets: "They've got everyplace else." That's the steel mills with their pipes and pumps. Lake Michigan has the look of a big dirty

103

bathtub in the midst of all that plumbing.

One evening in late summer, just before school was about to open, a few grade school children—white—were standing on a street corner at Fifty-first and Peoria. Some older youths —black—came up and told them to make way. During the dispute over who was going to keep the sidewalk, shotgun blasts were heard. A thirteen-year-old boy, who had been looking on from a porch swing a few doors off, was killed outright. A girl, also thirteen, was hit in the eye and died a few hours later. Both were white. The prosecution contends that they were incidental victims of a gang war, that the shots fired into their midst were aimed at the blacks by a rival gang. The slaughter of the innocents. It created a sensation—at the time.

It is a quarter to three before the court rises, the men and women of the jury file in and amply take their places. Since we are talking about black and white: there is one black woman on the jury, and a young Puerto Rican, very slight and small in his chair. The alternate sitting in the side box is black, white-mustached, hands stiffened atop his ball-headed cane. All the rest are white, more or less middle-aged: women in slacks, men in sport shirts, baseball jackets. A suggestion of leisure hours, domestic tasks; Saturday afternoon filling up shopping carts at the supermarket, trimming the grass. The defendants, at their table, return their glances with composure.

They are two slender young men, maybe twenty, twenty-one, dressed in high-heeled boots, vests, frock coats, satin cuffs, velvet collars. It's something of a shock. All their drama is in their dress. They look like something out of *Gone With the Wind*. In fact, they look like slave owners. You wonder how the jury, in the face of such incongruity, can form any impression of them. Ryan Murphy is handsome and bearded and props one boot casually on his knee. Cloyde Webb is serious and lean, his chin in his hand. The lenses of his glasses are like bubbles. They have been in county jail going on three years. The table is strewn with file folders, each six inches thick, stoutly labeled in laundry marker: MURDER. Each of the defendants has two lawyers, and there are two state's attorneys. There are more lawyers than spectators in the courtroom.

After seven weeks the prosecution has rested. The defense has just completed preliminary statements and will now begin to present its case.

First witness is a personnel supervisor at Spiegel's Inc., where Cloyde Webb worked. A fair stocky man who has spent the last couple of hours on the pay phone in the corridor, feeding it dimes, looking at his watch. I overheard him promising a succession of auditors that he was sure to give his testimony today. "I've been waiting all week." Now he seems anxious to get down to business, laying out the documents he has brought with him to be entered in evidence. An employee attendance record, a punched time card. He leans toward the microphone, peering over his glasses. The stenographer lifts her face expectantly, her wrists bent above the keys. Both are eying the lawyer at the lectern.

"And now, Mr. Rizzo, will you read for the ladies and gentlemen of the jury—*what is on that time card?*"

The state's attorney looks up from the table. "Objection!"

The defense lawyer asks for a side-bar.

Apparently this is a conference out of hearing of the jury. The judge steps down in his robes. The four defense lawyers and the two state's attorneys go into a huddle with him in the corner of the room. The court stenographer follows, embracing her stenotype machine. She is a very short perky black woman in a purple pants suit. You can barely hear the murmur

of their voices, but you can see her head poking sharply back
and forth, her fingers sinking away.

They resume their places. The stenographer lifts her gaze,
positions her hands.

"And now, Mr. Rizzo, do you happen to know *where Cloyde
Webb worked?*"

"Objection!"

The judge thinks for a minute. "Objection . . . overruled."

"You may answer."

"No."

"Is there any way you might *refresh your memory?*"

"Objection!"

"Objection . . . overruled."

Now it is the state's attorney's turn to ask for a side-bar.

Chairs totter, feet scrape. This time they all march off to the
judge's chamber, the little stenographer trotting at their heels.
Light pierces the edges of the frazzled window shades. The
men and women of the jury look at the defendants; the defendants look at the jury. Nothing passes between them.
There is something about a courtroom that effaces emotion—
expunges it. It's like a spell. Time has stopped. The courtyard
of Sleeping Beauty's castle; the fires long dead in the hearth,
the dogs and servants asleep. The large bailiff snorts a little,
head nodding forward, arms folded on his chest.

The door opens, the lawyers file briskly to the table. They
look angry—banging chairs, dropping pencils. As soon as they
sit down they all start scribbling away at their yellow pads. The
stenographer wriggles in her seat and loyally raises her eyes.

Mr. Rizzo is dismissed. He looks up: there must be some
mistake. Is that all there is to it? He hasn't had a chance to utter
one word of testimony. And the documents—he gathers them
up—worthless; they will never be entered in evidence now.
He grabs his hat and coat and edges toward the door, cautious,
not exactly relieved. He looks as if he wants to run.

The defense calls the next witness. A heavy young black woman takes her place in the box, pushing up her specs with her forefinger. The clerk shuts his eyes; up goes his sleeve:

". . . solemnly swear by the ever-livin' God . . ."

The state asks to approach the bench. The judge announces a short recess. It is half-past three.

A journalism student was sitting up front, a spiral notebook on his lap.

"Hey," I said. "You have any idea what's going on?"

He nodded promptly. "Yes. It's called bullshit. The defense objected all the way through the prosecution's case, so now it's their turn. That's how come this trial has been taking so long. The lawyers have used every delay in the book. And if that don't work they think up another. And with six of them—well, you can imagine. Someone's always late, or they don't show up altogether. I just feel sorry for the jury. You haven't seen anything yet. If you think this is something . . ."

A couple was sitting behind us. The woman leaned over the seat. "We thought maybe if they fined them," she said.

"Fines," her husband said, shrugging, without resentment. "Fines. Big deal. A lot they care."

They were the only other spectators. They belonged to the shopping bag. Both blond, roomy, blue-eyed; he wore a zippered windbreaker, she wore stretchpants and red lipstick. They were younger than they looked. In other words, their affiliation was stamped. She dropped her eyes when she said that she had known one of the dead children. "Ever since she was a baby."

They had been discussing the chart in front of the judge's bench; they seemed familiar with the layout of the houses on Green Street. I asked if they lived there. "Not any more," the husband said.

Chicago is the most segregated city in the country; that is its reputation. And it is true that to a great extent this is a matter of policy. Mayor Daley's neighborhood, Bridgeport, is a kind of museum; its composition, its crime rate—even rental prices—hark back to an earlier era. Practically the days of radio. It's that sort of dream. Urban life as a series of peaceful small towns: *Henry Aldrich, Fibber McGee and Molly, The Great Gildersleeve.* But that's the whole trouble; Chicago has never been integrated. Its constitution is basically suburban; homogeneous neighborhoods with well-defined borders; church parishes, company towns. When these barriers are breeched —when the dam bursts—when the bubble is popped—former residents flee. The great flat city—tarred rooftops stretching as far as the eye can see—has an appearance of squat stability. It looks solid, stolid, permanent. What were the temples and pyramids to our stockpiles of brick? But there is no real strength, no welding force. A city isn't just a lot of people. Or is it? This is a city of migrations. Our covenant is weak.

Mayor Daley had his own idea for revitalizing the sinking city. Shopping centers. They would be built in the midst of various neighborhoods and equipped with all the things you can find in a *suburban* shopping center. Cocktail lounges, bowling alleys, barbershops, movie theaters. So people would never have to leave home. The solution to isolation is more isolation.

The mayor's critics cracked up. (They used to think he was *funny.*) His grammar was bad—that's always good for a laugh, right? As if his constituents didn't talk the same way. In newsreel close-ups, jowly, clucking, he resembled a mourning dove. But obviously Da Mayor knew his home town—only too well. His scheme was true to its inner spirit. And his instinct was right; he put his finger on the problem. *Where are our sacred places?*

Now the diagram has been swung about to face the jury. The new witness is Lotis Roche. At the time of the murders, she was employed as an aide by the Chicago Police Department and lived in the house on the diagram with her mother, her sister, her five-year-old son, her twelve-year-old nephew. Both defendants lived in the house next door, owned by Ryan ·Murphy's stepfather, "Mr. Bob" Tunstall. In all, eleven people lived in that house.

"Miss Roche, are you a friend of Ryan Murphy's?"

"Yes."

"Did you visit him in jail?"

"Once."

"Did you write him a letter?"

"Yes."

"Miss Roche . . ." The defense counsel's voice has been dramatically rising. He's not exactly stout, but his chest is high, his cheeks firm and ruddy. He has crinkly blond hair; rings glitter on his fingers. Just now he flashes them like a smile with gold fillings: "Miss Roche, *would you lie for Ryan Murphy?*"

"Objection, judge!"

The state's attorney practically leaps to his feet, indignant, stung to the quick. He is what used to be called a *sheik:* pin-stripe suit, pale jaws, slick black sideburns. It seems there is bad blood between him and the defense counsel.

It was a Wednesday. Coming home from work, Lotis Roche got off the bus at Fifty-second and Halsted streets at 5 P.M., and the first thing she saw was "Ryan Murphy and Leota Watkins ridin' around on a minibike." (Objection.) Ryan was wearing beige pants and gym shoes. (Objection!) As soon as they caught sight of the witness, they chased her home on the minibike. (Objection!)

After supper she went out front to mow the grass. It was 6 P.M. Ryan Murphy waved to her from his minibike. He was on his way to a baseball game. He took his feet off the pedals and signaled with both hands.

"Was he still wearing the same thing?"

"Objection, judge! Can't you see how he's leading the witness?" The state's attorney flings down his pencil. The defense counsel turns to him with exaggerated politeness, rubbing his hands. "I'm surprised at you, Mr. Irving. Really very—"

"Gentlemen," says the judge.

Lotis Roche waits, patient, pushing up her specs on her nose with her finger.

"What did he have on?"

"Nothing except his beige pants and gym shoes."

Ryan Murphy grins, leaning back in his chair. Three witnesses have sworn they saw him holding a smoking shotgun. In police mug shots, with his face stiff-muscled and the number plate hanging from his neck, he looked sufficiently desperate. The way anyone looks in a police mug shot. (Boy, I'm glad they rounded him up. What a hard character. Look at those eyes.) But this is the first you have any actual glimpse of him. Somebody's neighbor, clowning on a minibike. Showing off: Look, Ma, no hands.

This matter of what did he look like, what was he wearing, is universal in criminal cases. It has to be; a question of identification. But in a contemporary courtroom, in a city like Chicago with its divided population, the eternal class struggle boiled down to black and white, the theme takes on a more oblique significance.

Example: An armed robbery trial. The prosecution is grilling the defendant about his hair style. During the period in question he had changed it several times—from processed to braided to natural. The prosecution seems to think he was trying to alter his appearance to avoid detection. The defendant maintains it was only fashion. And as a matter of fact, you

110

can see he's some dude. He has the good looks of a celebrity, a star athlete: tall, rangy, relaxed and lounging in the witness chair, the microphone intimately clasped in his knuckles. He exudes physical well-being, a natural superiority. He couldn't help it even if he wanted to. And for sure he doesn't want to. He seems patronizing, even a little amused, with the badgering questions, the pipsqueak lawyer. How often did he have to go to the barber with his natural? Every two weeks. How come he wore it combed some days, uncombed others? Because he felt like it. How long does it take for a process to grow out? Six weeks, maybe; all depends. (Hey, man, don't you know *nothing?*)

And the all-white jury. What are they supposed to make of this? How are they to judge? This is cultural shock.

"And what about that scar on your neck. You say you got it *on the tier?*"

Reticent—for the first time: "Someone scratched me."

"Someone stabs you. But you don't report it, you don't even go to the prison infirmary?"

"No, man. [Polite snicker.] You don't go reportin' every little old scratch you gits on the tier."

Example: Another armed robbery case. The lawyers are making summations to the jury. Two truckdrivers, uncle and nephew, had parked their rig in an alley. They heard rushing footsteps, a man running toward them with drawn gun. One turned to the other: "Oh, shit, here it comes."

The defendant is the size of a twelve-year-old. He wears a mustache, and his hair is brushed stiffly forward—a horn, a tusk. He seems absolutely frozen; his elbows are stuck to the arms of his chair. He was picked up shortly after the robbery for a traffic violation, wearing a black raincoat, like the robber. Both uncle and nephew pointed him out separately in the line-up. They had seen the gunman for perhaps thirty seconds in a dark alley.

111

The prosecution contends this is long enough. "You get a good look at a man if he's shoving a gun against your chest." To make his point, he proposes to count off thirty seconds for the jury—to pace it off, in front of them—staring all the while at his watch. All you can hear are his shoes creaking. The silence is stifling; it seems interminable.

The prosecution rests. It's up to the defense. But the defendant hasn't been much help. Arrested for armed robbery, he was unable to recall three days after where he had been at the time. Nothing. No alibi. He just keeps denying the charge. This has been going on for three years. So this must be a public defender too—it's not likely that the accused, putting up no defense, has hired his own counsel. This lawyer seems inexperienced enough—clumsy, repeating himself, haranguing the jury.

"I submit to you, ladies and gentlemen of the jury, I submit to you . . . I don't say they weren't robbed in that alley. I don't say that. But, ladies and gentlemen, I submit to you . . . [If he says it once more!] I submit to you: *How do you know this is the man?*"

He is rapidly and seedily balding; a mustache, long hair (except for the crown), bell bottoms, platform shoes. To be sure, the client has not given him much to go on. What more can he do but question the identification? And his argument is more powerful than it appears. It goes straight to the heart of the matter—what's barely left unsaid:

How do you know this is the man? How can you take their word for it? Could you be so sure? Come on—tell the truth. Don't they all look alike to you?

Most judges snap out their rulings. Objection sustained! Objection overruled! This one likes to think it over. He pushes out his lip in a sort of half smile and rolls up his eyes. Very unnerving. I went to school with him; he was a staid and senior member of a friend's fraternity. It seems to me that even then he had the same small slow judicious smile. Here, in a courtroom, it doesn't make him seem *fair*. It makes him seem arbitrary. You get the feeling he's only guessing.

Lotis Roche cut, raked and watered the grass. By that time it was getting dark. Some neighborhood boys were playing cards on the roof of Mr. Bob's white station wagon. (The state's attorney asks the stenographer to read back the names while he copies them out on his yellow pad. The defense counsel smiles down sardonically at the bent sleek black head —his hand on his hip; tapping his foot. His hair lifts and sticks out behind, same as his coattails.) Lotis Roche went into the living room and turned on TV. The clock above the set said 8 P.M. She switched channels around, watching first a bit of a John Wayne movie, then settling for *Medical Center*. While she was watching, she heard a shot. She ran to the window.

She steps down from the witness stand to tap the diagram with a pointer, indicating the location of the windows on Green Street. Her habit—pushing her specs up—makes her look prim and schoolteacherish.

"As soon as you heard the shot, you ran to the window?"

"Yes."

"And what did you see?"

"I seen the boys jumpin' off the station wagon and takin' off in all directions."

"Objection!"

"We know that as a police aide you were trained to shoot pistols. Now, was it a pistol shot you heard?"

"Objection!"

"Objection . . . overruled."

"No. It was a shotgun."

"Oh, so police aides learn to shoot shotguns too?"

"Objection!"

"Objection . . . overruled."

113

"No."

"But you were familiar anyhow with the sound of a shotgun blast?"

"Yes, sure, I heard them lots of times. When we lived in the projects, why we moved to Green Street. They was shootin' shotguns day and night."

"Objection, judge!" By this time the state's attorney is repeating it automatically, wearily, shutting his eyes, sulking in his seat. The defense counsel turns to the jury with a shrug, as if apologizing for a naughty child, holding up his hands. "Gentlemen. Please."

Lotis Roche went into the kitchen. Her mother was at the back door, talking to Mr. Bob. He was saying she should call the police. Objection. The mother called the police. Objection. A few moments later a squad car appeared; from the window she saw her mother leaning down and talking to the police. Suddenly they switched on the revolving light. They backed up over the sidewalk, swung the car around, sped off in the opposite direction—going the wrong way—down Green Street. Lotis Roche went back to watching *Medical Center.*

Next thing she knew, there was more flashing. She went to the window. All of Green Street was full of squad cars with streaking blue lights. Policemen were jumping out the doors, running across the lawns, pistols drawn. They were heading for Mr. Bob's house. Lotis Roche ran into her sister's bedroom; that window overlooked the side entrance of the house next door. The policemen stood there, trying to kick the door down. One looked up and saw the two women's heads sticking out the window.

She quotes him: " 'Niggers, you gonna get your heads blown off if you don't get back in.' "

"Did you and your sister go away then?"

"No; uh uh." Shaking her head emphatically. Her large

114

cheeks shudder. "We just went on hangin' out the window."

A few minutes later the police came out, dragging Ryan Murphy and pushing him along. He was wearing the same beige pants, "but only one gym shoe."

The judge declares a short recess. He calls the two lawyers to the bench. (Now they're gonna get it.) The jury files out, the defendants are marched away. The waddling bailiff brings up the rear, bangles of handcuffs dangling.

The two lawyers mutter with the judge. They turn away, cheerful. Two attractive young women have come in—thin, well dressed, smelling of make-up and perfume. They are the dates of the defense counsel and the state's attorney, and they all start talking about where to go for dinner, debating various noisy Greek restaurants on Halsted Street. They keep glancing toward the windows, as if they might be able to see and decide from here. Dusk lies radiant against the glass; the street lamps are glowing like pearls in champagne. Lines of traffic spangle the expressways—nervous twitching lights, all glittering and struggling toward the same source, the same goal, drawn by some image of lurid beauty.

The two men lounge against the table, the one in his pin stripes and sideburns, the other with his rings and crisp hair, evidently the best of friends. It was all an act; they were putting on a show. Lawyers have a license to carry on—to get emotional in a courtroom. They're the only ones. You can walk through any door. "Mr. Rubinstein, you are the rudest man I ever . . ." "In all my years of practice, Your Honor . . ." Etc., etc. They wag their heads, click their tongues, look daggers, slump in the seats. It's all faked, staged—part of their job; part of the game. Like the slamming sprawling brawls in the roller derby, the grunts and whacking mats in a wrestling match. It's a kind of canned belligerence. They make their living off aggression, don't they? It's a substitute for the violence that has brought them here.

Because there is nothing sensational about a courtroom. Nothing emotional. All that is checked at the door. The violence is spent; even the grief. There is something more powerful than individual feeling. I can't say what it is, but you can see that everyone knows it. Everyone senses that impersonal force, undemonstrative, undramatic, in all these rooms, crowded or empty. That is the only thing that everyone feels. That is the only meaning in the passive faces on the benches.

Back in Violence Court, the baby is still crying; feeble whimpers. The matron, frowning, her fists in thick white cuffs on her hips, tries to look disapproving, as if that will make it stop. The mother has been called to the witness stand. She hands the baby to the grandmother and knots her black lace under her chin. In the box, her face is distant, pale, expressionless, looking from one official to another.

There will be an interpreter. They pass the microphone back and forth.

"Were you at 2515 West 18th Street at approximately nine-forty on the night of . . ."

The interpreter repeats the question. The woman answers in rapid Spanish. The interpreter repeats her statement simply.

"Yes, at the door of my house."

"Objection."

"Where were you?"

"At the door of my house."

"Did you see Xavier Nuñez?"

"Yes, he came to my house asking for my husband."

"Objection."

"Did he ask for your husband?"

"Yes, at the door of my house."

"Did you notice at the time that he had a knife?"

"Objection."

"Did you notice anything unusual about Xavier Nuñez?"

116

"Yes. He had a knife. And he asked for my husband."

"He asked for your husband, the deceased Alberto Ortiz?"

The face in the box turns indifferently toward the noise of the questions, then toward the face of the interpreter. The grandmother paces under the window, the baby in her arms, bouncing it up and down in her black shawl. It's night outside. Across the aisle sits a vast Mexican woman, helplessly fat, sprawling on the bench like a turtle on its back. She is as expressionless as the other women. Is there some connection between them? Does she have anything to do with the case?

Slowly, stammeringly, the story comes out. This is the way it must be in a court of law—arcane knowledge in the hands of professionals. It's all a question of what you get to put in or leave out. The whole story is never told.

The husband came down the street that very moment and saw his wife standing in the doorway talking to Xavier Nuñez. The two men started arguing. They crossed the street together. The wife stood in the doorway, watching to see what they would do. She saw Xavier Nuñez raise his knife. A car passed and she lost sight of the two men. When she saw them again, her husband was down on the sidewalk. Xavier Nuñez, astride him, the knife in his hand, was raising his arm again and again.

Objection! Objection! Objection!

Again and again the two men cross the street together, the wife watches from the doorway. Again and again the knife flashes, the car passes, the husband goes down. The witness turns her head this way and that, her voice as flat, unemotional, as the interpreter's. God knows what she makes of all this; why they have to keep asking the same questions over and over. Can't they get a simple story right?

"Mrs. Ortiz. Do you see the man who stabbed your husband in this courtroom today?"

The interpreter starts to repeat the question. Before she can even get it out, the woman has swung swiftly about. Her arm extends straight before her; her finger shoots out at the end of her hand. She is pointing toward the defense table with a classic gesture of accusation. A young man in a black suit stiffens in his seat, tosses back his hair. For the first time you see his handsome profile: hooked nose, sable mustache. It's as if a flash of lightning had struck a tree. So this is why she has come, all she was waiting for. Just this. To turn on him, point her finger, avenge her wrongs.

It's an archaic moment in the courtroom.

GOLDEN AGE

Old Mrs. Alonzo, in a voice that scared the daylights out of you, called and asked me to come and see her in the Home. It was a gruff, deep billy-goat croak (male or female, you couldn't tell). I pictured her dark, lifted face, tarnished like a mirror; the light tilted in her glasses; her mouth open—as if that would help her to hear any better. The wire dangling from her hearing aid. So Professor Alonzo had finally put his old mother away.

I said, "Oh, Mrs. Alonzo," and she was flattered that I had recognized her over the phone.

I have an aged grandmother of my own, living on the other side of the city, so I used to look in on the professor's mother now and then. Feeling guilty; knowing it should have been the other old woman instead. The Alonzos' two flats perched one above the other in a deep court building, the yard bushy with trees. They were identical: grottoes. His furnished in books, top to bottom; leather library chairs, brass nailheads, the curdled fumes of cigars and whiskey decanters. The life of the mind was masculine turf. Hers was a matter of bric-a-brac, lace doilies, shaky-legged tables, and snarled faded carpets which reminded me of the worn hair on the back of her head. The TV set was often blaring full blast; which didn't distract her in the least—she couldn't hear it. She pressed her hand to her noisy bosom, breathing rapidly and loudly. You couldn't restrain a sense of alarm—as if something were breathing down your neck.

Now, the old lady loved to brag about her son—bald, stout, sixtyish, rough and scolding in manner, red in the face. With a great air of taking me into her confidence, seizing my arm and whispering, she showed me his clippings. "He's a famous man, you know." Well, he was, he was, much more than she thought. What could his dry-as-dust essays mean to her? What could she make of them? Written at white heat, in a hand that sent secretaries up the wall. Did you expect her to believe that anyone actually read such stuff?

In the dim light her glasses glittered—a mother's skeptical pride.

With Alonzo, alas, it was another story. He practically had to shout at her, at the top of his voice. She couldn't make out a word he said. I don't know; she always seemed to understand me. Of course, such commonplaces as we exchanged . . . Still, the great professor could speak commonplaces too:

"Mother, I'm going home now," he'd announce, rising, pushing thick fingers into pockets of tweed. The leather-patched sleeves smelled of Irish pubs and English fogs.

"What's that? What's that?" Opening her mouth, lifting her head. Her wires tingling.

He raised his voice. "I say. I'm go-ing home. Now. Down-stairs."

"What? What? Huh? What's that?"

She lifted her face, he bent his; the two faces—so much alike, two swelling gourds, rimless specs stuck on the noses—pushing closer and closer. His was getting redder and redder —froggy-eyed. I was afraid he was going to have an attack. But that's what I was always afraid of. Bluster was Alonzo's trademark; he shouted down everybody. His brilliance bordered on apoplexy. Its effects were famous on three continents. In the heat of argument, he actually seemed to lisp; his breath whistled between closed lips, and his hair looked like thistles. You couldn't help getting scared for him, once he got started.

His old mother croaked and cocked her head, her innocent specs flashing. She looked like Little Orphan Annie with the frizz of curls, the silver-dollar eyes. Meanwhile cowboys on the television were shooting off their cap pistols. Take that—and that—and that. You saw puffs of smoke.

This was a routine, of course. They were hamming it up.

Burlesquing their relation, since it had become a burlesque. Doting mother, dutiful son. But their roles had been painfully reversed. Now it was her turn to play the slow stubborn creature who needed to be reasoned with, looked after, coaxed; now he was the one who had his hands full. At one end of life and the other, still the same gap. No understanding. So he hollered and lisped, she shook her deaf ear. They expressed their connection. There must be a better way of saying it, with someone you love, who won't be around much longer. But no one seems to have hit upon it yet.

Mrs. Alonzo was recovering from a heart attack. Then she started falling. The professor, at his desk, heard the thumps downstairs. She was supposed to knock on her floor—his ceiling—if she wanted anything. But no. She got out of bed by herself instead and groped her way to the bathroom. All the solid old-fashioned fixtures—painted pipes, grouty tiles, Roman faucets— waiting to crack her bones. He listened to every creaking overhead, and imagined her tripping on her shabby carpets.

She was giving him a hard time; people give what they can.

I saw for myself how things were going. A friend paid a visit with his son. The little boy took a look around—one room yawning into the other, the light receding, the brittle lace yellowing on armchairs and tables—and in a small voice asked Mrs. Alonzo how old she was. The old lady lied about her age —lopped off ten years. (Why ten? Why be stingy? Why not twenty?) Then she wanted to hold his hand. She reached for it, clawing—they were side by side on the boggy sofa—as if she meant to snatch it away.

"It's mine, it's mine. I'm going to keep it."

She wasn't kidding. Her voice was sharp, her fingers pinched. The child stiffened, but let his hand lie in hers. I watched this with very big eyes—almost as big as his.

"Actually I don't like old people," he told me. "They give me shivers up my spine."

I guess I'm talking about the shivers.

As long as this lovely spell of Indian summer holds, you see the old people sitting outside every day on the park benches by the underpass. A curving sweep of grass, squirrels pouncing on leaves, traffic wincing on the Outer Drive. The blue blue shimmer of Lake Michigan. Beyond, the tall downtown buildings docked on the horizon, ready to sail on. At each bench sits a wheelchair, a "senior citizen" within; and on the bench—shackled like some familiar spirit—a sturdy black woman with her knitting, or a movie magazine spread open on her knees. They come from the Shoreland, Sherry-Netherland, Del Prado, Windermere—hotels once famous for ballrooms, dance bands, steak houses, now providing package care for the elderly. My favorite of these couples is an old gent with a hooked back, a hound's-tooth check cap and plus-fours and his young pregnant nursemaid. He likes to get out of his chair and push; she dawdles at his side. Her belly lifts the front of her coat; her legs look gray in white stockings. Meanwhile the great yellow maple is shaking its branches, squandering leaves. They scatter like petals. It's raining beauty; the air is drenched with gold.

Empty folding chairs were still standing out, all up and down the front walk of the Woodlawn Nursing Home. A skinny, straggling line-up, as if the old folks themselves were sitting and staring. It had been another warm fall day; bright crab apples strewed the lawn and the leaves were swirling. Coming round the bend, I could already hear voices like Mrs. Alonzo's—raucous, growling in a drainpipe.

"Well, what about these teachers of yours?" a man was

saying. "These Arthur Murray teachers? Were there any women at least?"

He was very small, very neat, with a tight white collar, a tight brown skin. His lip was stretched against his tight white teeth.

"Oh, no," from his companion, a woman leaning on a stick. "Only men. Two men."

"Men," he said. "Thanks a lot. Who needs that?"

The home is built in two wings—a tall one, where the inmates live, and a long low entrance wing with waiting rooms and administrative offices. The corridors were smooth, gleaming, done in Howard Johnson colors—turquoise and orange —and a *sukkah* stood in the lobby. It was real. Red oak leaves, Indian corn, yellow squash, lemons, oranges, apples, melons. A woman saw me sniffing at the fruit and motioned for me to help myself. She was large and soft, smiling from cheek to cheek, and her lips squeaked, soundless, as if you'd squeezed rubber. Take, take. But I didn't take.

Another woman, with a cane and dark glasses, was sitting sideways in her chair and asked for the time without looking up.

I stopped to read the bulletin board. There seemed to be a heavy schedule. Movies, cocktail parties, religious services, bingo, Arthur Murray. A woman was pushing herself along in a wheelchair and stopped to see what I was looking at.

"They keep you pretty busy here?" I said.

"No-o-o," she said slowly, thinking it over and gazing up at the board. She asked what time it was.

It was four-thirty; getting close to dinner. That's why everyone was so interested in the time. Meals come early in institutions, remember—a matter of kitchen shifts. It was too early to go, but everyone was ready. All along the corridor, they were waiting in their chairs, asking each other the time. Some were already sitting in the dining room, at small tables with red-checked cloths. Steely carts. Prominently displayed was a juice machine, the sort you see in movie theaters, popcorn galleries, stroking and churning a thick purple froth.

The dining room was in the other wing. As soon as you stepped over the border, the scene changed in an instant. Everything was older, darker, glummer, more dingy. The corridors were dim and narrow and lined with chairs, like the gloomy hallways of a clinic. And there was the familiar clinging urinal smell. Leaky bladders? Old people missing the pot? This was where they lived, that's all. That was the difference.

I got into the elevator and rode upstairs. Same thing there; everywhere the old people were converging. Tapping down the halls on canes, holding onto the handrails on the walls, propping their shiny chrome walkers before them. They came rolling up in their wheelchairs, elbows lifted, working, gristly grasshopper wings. Passing open doorways, I could see women—they were mostly women—leaning over sinks, looking into mirrors, primping for dinner.

Mrs. Alonzo was not one of these. I knew she was bedridden, had brought her some books and a magazine which had just published a piece of mine—she liked to read. From the doorway, however, I saw that she was asleep; cranked up in bed against a pile of pillows, the rails raised on either side. Her head was back, her mouth was slack, and the string was hanging from her earpiece. Her breathing sounded as if a prowler had broken in, ransacking, rummaging round in her chest.

Just then the nurse came in to give her a pill. The old woman's eyes flew open behind rimless specs—a startled expression, a sort of angry surprise. Her head struggled up. She gasped something down from a little paper cup. The nurse went out, hips wagging in her girdle.

The Home is in the thick of a desolate black slum. Burned out, bombed out, boarded up. Charred timbers, rubble, shattered windows. Through the slats of Venetian blinds I spied

125

children playing stickball in an empty lot. It was planted like a minefield with bricks, stones, scrap metal, squinting glass. In other words, what is called these days "the inner city." What a confession. Well, what can you do when civilization itself goes into competition with you—sets up its own spectacles of decline and destruction? Here was an old soul under the wrecking ball, undergoing the same kind of senseless assault. It was plain she had no idea who I was. (Who was I?) I pulled up a chair and sat down by the bed, my magazine under my arm.

The old woman looked over and stared at me, eyes wide open, as if something had her by the throat. She tried to lift her head. Her mouth munched. She was asking for something; thought I was the nurse. "What is it? Water?" I held the glass tube to her lips. She wouldn't drink. "You want your pillows straightened? You want to be turned?"

She kept trying to speak, straining her head. Then she gave a loud burp. Her throat rasped. I thought she was going to spit up the pill she'd just taken, and fetched the bedpan and held it to her chin. But that wasn't it either. I was getting panicked, ready to yank the bell for the nurse.

The fact is, I was frightened at being left alone with her, as I had been frightened my first time alone with a newborn infant. Not knowing what it wanted, what it needed. Its tottering head, its grasping fingers. I was frightened and ashamed of myself for not knowing what she wanted. Or, rather, for continuing to ask, to seek . . . as if. As if there actually were something—anything—a simple measure, word, gesture that would do. And that would be "what she wanted."

Her hand reached over the rail, feeling for my hand. The gesture seemed feeble, but the grip was strong. I remembered the way she had grabbed, grasped the little boy's hand. Her eyes were faded, the irises surrounded by dim thick rings. Aureoles. This truly reminded me of the newborn infant: two

126

staring eyes, "clouds of glory." Some tenuous connection with the other world. I looked back, wondering and wondering. Is it a puzzle—or a mystery?

"Ma," she said. Then she sighed. "Oh, boy. Gosh. Oh, gee whiz."

My mother had just started to work for the Golden Diners Club, a program for "senior citizens" from the mayor's office. There are more than fifty throughout the city, where the elderly can get "hot, nourishing, low-cost lunches." They pay what they like; they don't need to pay anything. It isn't charity or welfare, it isn't only for the poor. But it is hard to convince people, especially the ones who need it most. The ones who are not used to taking, who have not much left but their pride. They don't owe anybody anything; they have paid their dues.

My mother works in a synagogue on the North Side, where they serve kosher food; so the customers are almost all Jews, from the old country, more or less religious. We were going to a funeral in the family and had arranged to meet there at lunchtime. In the meantime my mother sent me in her car to fetch her lazy old aunt, Yetta, who sometimes comes to eat.

Auntie Yetta lives only a few blocks away, in a terrace of brick two-flats right next to the concrete bunker of the el tracks. The trains go past like a rock slide. It looks like a munitions factory. Crab grass shoots from cracks in the concrete, the bricks, the cement sidewalk. How heavy-hearted the smell of the warm autumn day, rising from all this mortar. So it seemed to me.

It took Yetta a long time to come to the door. Then I could hear her unfastening the many locks and chains. All my grandmother's sisters look alike—like their mother, The Bobbe. When I think of my great-grandmother, I see the scanty rusted grass on the slight mound of her grave, the tipping headstone. Then there rises before me the great leaning form of The

Bobbe herself, pitching her weight heavily from side to side.

The old woman had trouble with her legs; thick, swollen, bowed—from ankle to knee it was a forty-five-degree angle. I'm not exaggerating. She went without a cane, but her walk was listing and broken. All her daughters have the same difficulty; it's an ethnic disease, like sickle-cell anemia or Tay-Sachs syndrome, and afflicts women of the East European diaspora. A very exclusive Jewish disease. The thighbone softens and bends and drags you down like a fruit tree. Of course, I didn't know this as a child; their distorted legs were just them, the way they looked—how, I thought, they were supposed to look. Or, as I would say now, characteristic. Even more characteristic were their Slavic cheeks—wide, flat, heavy with bone. They seemed to peer at you over a ledge: above, you saw the glitter of eyes. They all looked like squatting idols, gazing at you from a distance. So maybe I am imagining The Bobbe, wide in her chair, filling it from side to side—huge, silent, her hands heavy on the armrests, and her terrible legs in front of her, wrapped in sleeves of flesh. Maybe.

She wore gypsy scarves, earrings, beads; she was, virtually, a gypsy. Her house was always full of her cronies, with their cards and tea leaves, rolling their little brown cigarettes with a flick of the tongue—all their gold teeth twinkling like loot. They cracked dirty jokes (according to my mother) in the Romany dialect. I do remember the heads together, laughing. But I can't recall that The Bobbe ever said a single word to me. I didn't speak any of her languages. Besides, it must have got boring after a while—all those descendants. Thirty grandchildren; so she must have stopped counting the great. Give an old woman a break. It's thirty years ago now; she slipped and fell in the bathtub, cracked her hip, couldn't get out. The water turned cold. She died of pneumonia a week later. A series of events I regret to this day.

The door opened and there stood white-haired Auntie

Yetta, more conservative than her mother—as who wouldn't be?—but with the same prominent cheeks, flat barriers, the same legs sinking under the weight of her body. She gazed at me over her cheekbones. She was still in her slip.

"Oh, I can't go; I'm sick today, honey," she said. Whining a little. I could see this was a lot of hooey. She just didn't feel like getting dressed. Not in the cards. In that family they never cared to get dressed. As a child I used to love to stay overnight for a visit, so I wouldn't have to get dressed either. Behind her, the room was in a familiar mess; clothes, newspapers strewn everywhere, dirty dishes, bread crusts, banana peels, apple cores. It's always like that, since Yetta also doesn't care to clean. If you were a fish, you could swim through it. She wades; sidewise, clutching—a slow crustacean.

Yetta told me that another sister, Hodl, might be going to the Golden Diners today. Hodl had taken her husband to the clinic in the morning and they would be coming from the el. "You should keep an eye out; you might spot them."

It was actually hot; lawn mowers buzzing, spraying fine green dust. It was almost like spring, though the air smelled of leaf smoke. I didn't see anyone on the way. I was in the bathroom at the *shul,* washing my hands at the sink before lunch, when a white-haired woman came hauling herself in, lurching from side to side. She wore a cotton housedress zipped up the front; her legs were curved, her cheeks stone slabs.

"Auntie Hodl."

She put her fingers to her forehead. "Oh, I know who you are," she said. "I know who you are."

She was worn out. She had taken her husband to the clinic at 7:30 A.M. and they had just got back. "You know how they keep you waiting." He has dizzy spells, faints all the time, for some reason can walk only backward. So it would have been easy enough to "spot them" coming down the street, him toppling backward and her from side to side. In this manner, the two sick old people get themselves where they have to go. They climb the stairs of the elevated tracks and board crazed rushing trains. How does she shove him on? I wonder. This has been going on for years.

One hundred and sixty-seven had signed up for lunch today; only so-so. Fridays the turnout is better; then they can expect *challah,* wine, roast chicken. Today no one knew what was on the menu, and everyone was asking. A typical church function room: a platform at one end, windows narrow and high up, the dull gleam of linoleum and long tin-topped tables; the clatter of metal chairs. At each place was laid a slice of bread in a wax-paper pocket; a paper napkin, plastic knife, fork and spoon, and a slice of pineapple in a plasticized cup. The faces of the clientele too seemed remarkably standardized. It was the false teeth and the glasses: they lent a kind of artificial light. Their eyes looked so big, they seemed to explode behind thick lenses. The old people sat like a new race of children, lifting up their big blurred eyes. They were waiting for the prayer.

An arm shot up in the back of the room, waving a paper napkin. My father, signaling to me to show where we were sitting. So he's talking to me today. A great mauled-looking man in a dark-blue suit. It was the latest style, single-breasted, narrow in the shoulders, belted in back, and every time he made one of his large gestures, I was sure he'd rip a seam. This Lord Fauntleroy stuff is not for him. I'd say Dying Gladiator or Laocoon. His skullcap sat on the back of his thick dusty hair like a lid; his shirt collar and tie looked to be choking him, and his eyes were a startling, smarting, blinking blue—like the eyes of a coal miner emerging from the pits.

My father always looks startled—you would too, if you'd

been born in the wrong century—but today he looked stricken. There was a glare behind his glasses. The death was in his family—a beautiful child.

Everyone gets frightened, hearing of the death of a child. Everyone knows what it means: a puncture pain, a hook in the heart. We say "heartache," "heartbreak," the heart this and the heart that. But the strange thing is, that's really where you feel it. Wonder what that means.

One of my parents' closest friends, the companion of many years, had been murdered about a week before. Not even a robbery: two men walked into his store and asked for him by name. "You Zuckerman?" "Yes; what can I do for you?" So they shot him seven times. The period of mourning was just over, the widow wearing dark glasses to hide swollen eyes, talking slowly, tonelessly in a voice hollow with sedation, a chain of thick gold rings, bracelets, hanging heavy from her neck: the jewelry on her husband's hands when he died. Hal Zuckerman always went in for jewelry. Heavy-set, bald and round-faced as Churchill, smoking big green cigars. (They seemed to me, as a child, to turn the air green around him.) Even in those days—he was not always as prosperous as he looked—he sported thick gold bolts on his fingers. I think my father would as soon wear a ring in his ear. But I guess you could say his "heart" was heavy.

Across the table were Auntie Hodl and Aunt Sylvia—it was her day off; she was going with us to the funeral. In the meantime, my mother had been putting her to work. "She always finds something for people to do." Sylvia, the younger, thinks her older sister is bossy. We both looked at my mother, dashing about, radiantly white-haired in her light blue pants suit. Her hair was whiter than anyone's here. Next to her empty place, a large, loose-jointed man leaned on his elbows, smoking. There was a No Smoking sign over his head, and his long-jawed face was wreathed in jolly fumes. Smoke poured from his hairy ears and spurted from his nostrils. He reached over and nipped my mother's bread.

The microphone gave a piercing bleat and whistled. A young woman stood on the platform, asking for "everyone's attention." But everyone hadn't come to give their attention. Their manner—necks stretching, fists on the table—said plainly enough that they had come to *get*. Where were the eats? They were growing impatient. Meantime she was announcing the day's activities and the circulation of a petition. A bill proposing abolition of the state sales tax on food, for senior citizens. (In Illinois there is a tax on food.)

No one was listening, and the microphone seemed to pop with exasperation.

"If you don't care about yourselves, no one will care about you," she said.

I didn't hear the prayer, but someone must have said it, because people were chewing their bread. And the man with the fur in his ears ripped off my mother's pineapple.

Two women, evidently Golden Diners themselves, were pushing their way along the rows of chairs, one fearfully lifting a tray of little soup bowls. The liquid was trembling; you could see the golden *mandeln* bobbing up and down in the broth. The other functionary, following close behind, seemed to be doing nothing but scolding shrilly at the first one.

"Oh, no, not again," my father said, ducking his head. "Better watch it. Those two dizzy dames are always at it. Fight fight fight."

They slapped the bowls on the table; the soup spilled and ran all over my mother's chair. "Look what you did, you did," the loud one squawked, screeching and flapping.

"Don't yell at her so much," I said. "You make her nervous."

"Don't pay no attention to her, darling," the first one said, rolling her eyes at me over her shoulder. "You got to feel sorry; she's not all there."

So the little bowls slopped and splashed on the tables. Don't spill the soup, the soup. The microphone shrieked and hooted. My father bent down, mopping up my mother's chair with paper napkins. The old guy neatly snatched away her soup plate.

Sitting next to Auntie Hodl was a man who looked familiar. A beaming circle of a face, his napkin tucked round his chin. His eyes in big glasses stared owlish and unblinking. Out of the corner of my eye, I thought I saw Hodl twisting toward him now and then—giving him a sharp poke, a tap on the wrist, or swiping his chin. It dawned on me that she was "minding" him—that this must be her husband, Uncle What-sisname. Now we were even.

I was wondering about something. My mother and her sister Sylvia are a handsome pair. Not smart, expensive women; they're working-class wives who get their hair done every other week, and manicures maybe once or twice a year, for special occasions. (Except they would call them "affairs.") They don't shop at Field's, let alone Saks, and they go in for shiny fabrics and bright colors—the pinks, purples, yellows, oranges, greens, preferably all at once—of their Romanian grandmother. Especially purple. *Nor spring nor summer beauty hath such grace/As I have seen in one autumnal face.* The two sparkling silver sisters get dressed up, go to weddings, and put the brides to shame. (It's true my mother has her grim, dark, liverish days, but I'm not talking about that now.) My mother is older by some eight or nine years, and leads an even livelier social life. She's always stepping out. "Where's your mother tonight?" my grandmother wants to know whenever I call. She thinks I keep tabs. "Is that a Jessie! Always running."

Okay. My point is this. My white-haired mother could be one of those sitting and waiting at these tables herself—not working here. Auntie Hodl is only six or seven years older, and look at the life she leads. And how resignedly. A waddling old woman with a sick husband in tow, wiping his nose. She seems to have no complaint to make, no other set of expectations. Then what is the difference? What constitutes entry into the ranks of the elderly? Where is the dividing line, if it's not just years. Money? There must be more to it. Sickness? Senility? Being alone? But Hodl has children; grandchildren too. I bet they all do. The people at the Woodlawn Home have families: it's their families that put them there.

In my neighborhood I pass a certain basement window, Council for the Jewish Elderly. You see signs: Do you need a lawyer? A doctor? A visiting nurse? Information about Medicare? Medicaid? Hours are posted for the shuttle-bus service to Michael Reese Hospital. It looks like they've got troubles. The elderly are a subculture in our society of subcultures. That is, they have not so much a life in common as a condition. Who understands this condition? What can be made of it? Cut off, under attack, no retreat.

These people were all old Jews. Judging from the accents I heard around me, most of them had come over on the boat. They were not, as the jargon goes, assimilated. But there are places like this all over the city. Golden Diners—Golden Agers—are not just immigrant Jews. And yet their status is symbolic. This is no country for old men. All of them must be in the same boat; they are not entirely of America either.

Our party was attracting attention. Faces were turning on us enviously from all the other tables. Privileged characters. They didn't like to see outsiders here in the first place. And now we were getting served first, to top it all off, while they sat waiting. (My mother had told them in the kitchen that we had to go to a funeral.) The two bickering old biddies were making their way toward us again, bringing the main course

—the trays held high, as if to keep them out of reach. The one was still timidly hiding her head, the other still yelling, stretching the veins in her throat. For once the buzz in the room died down; people stiffened into silence.

"Who's going to the fu-ner-al?" she was demanding, at the top of her voice. "Who's going to the fu-ner-al?"

Scolding, to the old, must seem a way of life. We all scold my grandmother too. How come she never keeps the chain up on the door? Why won't she use a cane? When will she let someone take her to the doctor? Etc., etc. She's eighty-five, crippled with arthritis, a widow on a pension of something like a hundred dollars a month. So who do we think we're kidding, with our canes and doctors and door latches? Who's she going to fool with that stuff? She ducks her head and lets us talk.

It's in Uptown, a large old elevator building. In Chicago, a city of the plains, built outward, low-lying, such vintage structures are not so common. This neighborhood, now so squalid, was once fancy: stone urns on the lintels, potted geraniums, doormen in gold braid. A mayor of Chicago used to live here. At least, every time we enter and traverse the vast lobby—a trackless waste; I feel like a camel plodding across the Gobi Desert—my father remarks: "Mayor So-and-so of Chicago used to live here." (I met this Mayor So-and-so once, was taken up to the dark wood-paneled offices with their swinging gates and swivel chairs, golden windowshades, rich green blotters. I had won a grade school spelling bee. The mayor pushed out his hand—past his big, buttoned paunch—and, as we shook, asked me to spell "eleemosynary." I corrected his pronunciation. My God.) (I was wrong.) I don't know where my father gets his information, and I'm not sure what he means. But I have an idea. He means that every dog has its day.

And in fact this neighborhood will rise again; it's in the path of progress, so to speak. Heading north along the lakefront, the trail of the young, the fashionable, the singles bars, wine and cheese shops, liberal politicians, psychiatrists' town houses. The culture mishmash—propagandists for the good life in the city. ("Interesting people with complex demands," as one of the rental ads puts it. God forbid anyone should admit to simple needs.) First there was Old Town, then New Town; next will be Uptown. It's inevitable. And the drive must be very great—it must be all-powerful—to overcome even this. The decrepit old buildings with their jagged windows and smell of leaking sewer gas will come down; glass high rises will go up in their place; the misery will move elsewhere. That part is easy; it travels; it's foot-loose and fancy-free.

The lobby is stripped; just a few cracked mirrors, prongs in the chandeliers where the lights used to be. At one end a black-and-yellow sign: FALL-OUT SHELTER. It leads upstairs; that makes me wonder. Down at the other end, the glassed-in reception desk, a shirt cardboard leans against the counter, scribbled in pencil: OUT TO LUNCH. Through the window you can still see the old-fashioned switchboard, plugs torn from the sockets; the empty pigeonholes which used to hold mail, telegrams, important worldly messages. The present tenants get mail once a month: pension, relief checks. The desk clerk has been out to lunch for fifteen years.

The *pièce de résistance* is the elevator. There are two, one reserved for the janitor's use. As you can see, someone has a sense of humor. Janitor? What janitor? And since none exists, do we need to invent one? The tenants are not here to complain about leaky faucets. They're on their last legs themselves, a condition they are used to. My uncle was trapped in this elevator once; it fell to the basement, the door wouldn't open and the alarm didn't work. What else is new? He hollered and banged until the Fire Department finally came to the

136

rescue. A cop, six foot four, padded with police fat; he didn't think it was funny. And what if it had happened to one of *them?*

The upper part of the door is a dirty gray slush color; through the glass, if that is what it is, you can see the light coming: rising like an acetylene torch in a mine shaft. The elevator clanks, creaks, rattles its chains, scrapes and lashes overhead like storm-tossed branches. This is it in a nutshell, a capsulized version of our city life—its paranoia, its guilt and dread. An ancient, corrupt piece of machinery, plainly a fire hazard, no sticker of inspection. Is it going to fall? Is it going to fail? Will the door open? And who will get in? Some drunk breathing fumes you could light with a match. A quarrelsome derelict. Or just someone so old, so broken-down, so weary of the march, you hate to look. You drop your eyes. That's the worst part. I would take the stairs, but it's ten flights up and they're not always lighted. Groping my way down once, striking matches, I came upon a pair of broken glasses in a pool of dried blood. As for the freight elevator, never send to know. . . .

This building is ten times better than the one my grandmother moved out of a few years ago.

At your knock, you hear her slippers shuffling to the door. The chain scrapes in the latch. She opens and peeks out, head thrust forward, peering from the hump between her shoulders.

"How many times do I have to tell you? First you look—then you take the chain off the hook. What good does it do if you take the chain off before you open?"

"I know, I know."

She knows.

Her feet scrape the floor, dragging along the big loose slippers. Big swollen hands dangling from her wrists. She flaps one. "Leave the door open for some air. It's all right now you're here."

Her voice croons. From Transylvania, she moved to Kentucky. It's not enough my grandmother is half gypsy; she has to be a hillbilly too. But never mind family history. The bed is made, the table cleared, dishes are stacked in the drain rack. She's not like her sister Yetta. Still, you don't have to be nosy to see it's not so clean either. The dishes are greasy, the floor could use sweeping, there's a smell from the bathroom like the odor in the corridors of the Woodlawn Home. A drizzle of soot from the open window, the curtains struggling and fluttering. A row of pickle jars on the sill, filled with cloudy water; sprouting sweet potatoes, wandering Jew—the thin strings of roots reaching in all directions—a cracked avocado pit thrusting up one scrawny shoot. No power on earth could keep these windows clean. Chicago lies before us in all its unfinished business. Brightness falls from the air.

"Well? How are you feeling?"

"I?" Turning herself, stiff-necked, sideways. Surprised you should ask. "I'm all right."

"Then what took you so long to make up your mind?"

She chuckles. This is our form of communication, like Alonzo and his mother with their vaudeville routine. I can't say when we got into this habit, but after all, she knows what I mean. I guess she knows. I hope so. Because it's a little late, now, to start delivering messages. To bring up the one subject, the real subject. You have to begin that in time. Otherwise it sounds too much like last things. And I sometimes think she is a little afraid of me; that she senses, through the banter, that I might suddenly start talking in another vein. What then? She has never been the demonstrative type. Never one to volunteer information. She's not going to be the one to bring it up, sitting in her corner, her hands heavy in her lap.

My grandmother's fingers are bent—fused—in the shape of a priest making the sign of the cross. Pretty strange, huh, for an old Jewish lady with all her Jewish infirmities. With these hands she pries open tins, digging at the jagged lids with an old-fashioned puncture-type opener—the kind I can't use. The only kind she can. She has no grip. She carries food to the table, hot heavy pots practically dangling from her fingertips. Her shoulders pulled up, her head pulled down. Now, what would she say if she knew I was thinking all the while that she looked like the Pope?

No sooner have we sat down, the door open, than in slinks a black cat, arching and rubbing itself along the wall. Presently two women approach, holding onto one another, hand in hand.

"Did anyone see a cat?"

Their voices quaver. They appear to be identical twins—is this possible? Two withered old crones, crooked backs, hooked noses. Even their chins are hooked, tipping upward—hoops. White hairs quiver on their chinny-chin-chins. To top it all off, they're dressed like twins; dolled up, perhaps, by some doting mother—knitted caps, crocheted shawls, thick woolen socks and Mary Janes with buckled straps. The impression is overpowering. This must be what is meant by second childhood.

"A black cat?"

"Look under the bed," says my grandmother.

That's what she always used to say whenever I asked her for a penny. She wasn't being facetious—not her style. Her husband, my grandfather, was a big handsome man, a storekeeper, careless with small change. It fell out of his pockets, got stuck in his shoes, his trouser cuffs, and when he undressed at night, rolled around on the floor. So if I crawled under the bed I could strike it rich. In those days my grandmother was big and handsome herself—pardon me for bragging—five foot nine, astonishing for a turn-of-the-century East European immigrant. She wore her dark hair divided in the middle, combed in two large flat rolls above her temples. With her wide-set eyes, wide impassive cheeks, it gave her a look of powerful repose.

"Sit down," my grandmother offers. "He'll come out when he's ready." The black curve of the tail was sticking out from under the bedspread. The aged twins, plucking at each other, steadying, holding hands—at the same time helping and hindering—tiptoe in and pull out chairs at the table.

I suppose I should say something about the furniture. It's in keeping. Junk. An enamel-topped kitchen table, scratched, like a bathtub; a dining room set; a couple of "upholstered" chairs—sprung, soggy stuff you wouldn't be surprised to find in an alley. Which is probably where my father found it. And by the way—where do all those busted, waterlogged sofas and mattresses come from, that I keep seeing on the curbs these days? Is there an epidemic?

In other words, this is not, as with Mrs. Alonzo, the accumulation of a lifetime. There is scarcely anything here from the past. My grandmother does not go in for souvenirs. Sylvia has told me many a time how, even in the old days, with a houseful of kids, the whole family packed up and moved every two years—without fail. So they could get the free decorating when they signed a new lease. There is a television set, of course, rabbit ears sticking up, and a telephone at last—a Christmas gift from Sylvia. Now we can worry when we ring and ring and get no answer.

The twins have a story. It seems they had found a pension check in the street, under the viaduct that leads to Foster Beach. (I know the spot—like a slaughterhouse with its feathers and pigeon splash.) At first, they had passed it up.

"But I told Sis right away, I sez, 'Say, if that don't look like a pension check.' Did I say that or didn't I?"

"I could of told you. Anyone could reckonize a pension check. It's the govverment onvelope."

"So we went back and picked it up."

Went back. That would be worth a discussion. It's not so easy to "go back"—to retrace such doubtful, painful, tottering steps. Each one takes so much effort. What if it wasn't a check? What if it was torn open, empty? But there it was, the address nearby. Trembling, all excitement, the twins looked up the rightful owner. A colored man named Jackson. He came downstairs in his overalls; he was working on the roof.

"You Jackson?"

"What do you want to know for?"

The story was getting exciting. My grandmother meantime listening, turning sideways, her shoulders lifted to her ears. Her glasses flashing with a candid light. The way she listens to everybody, keeping her thoughts to herself.

Jackson, for reward, gave them five bucks apiece. And oh, you should see what they bought with it at the A & P. More than they could carry. I'll bet. The elderly, who can afford it the least, buy the most expensive way—the smallest quantities. There are lots of reasons. Because they're alone, they're afraid they won't use it up, they have to watch their money, there's no place to put the stuff. And, not the least, they have to get what they can carry. No use picking out a five-pound bag of sugar if you can't lift five pounds. They have to think of that; a prominent fact of life in these parts. Once I arrived just as my grandmother was coming along in her bright-green coat —head poked forward in her babushka, her legs so bent they seemed dragged down by the heavy package weighting either hand. She was carrying a bundle for her neighbor. It occurred to me that anyone noticing her—if anyone notices anyone here, where they all have such grim preoccupations of their own—a stranger, passing, would think: Here comes a funny little old lady. An elf, a gnome. And not know. Know what? What am I trying to say?

And what was she doing carrying someone else's groceries? Well, I could believe these twins had struggled with their miserable shopping bags, ten bucks' worth of food, putting them down and lifting them up and tugging at each other's sleeves all the way home. They went on talking.

I used to resent these gate-crashers. Every time I pay a visit to my grandmother, someone else shows up. It never fails. The next-door neighbor, for instance, picks just this moment to return the *TV Guide.* (Sylvia's husband, a printer, works for the paper and keeps the old lady in *TV Guides.*)

"Oh, I didn't know you had *company,*" the neighbor will say, clutching and closing her wrapper. "I'll come back later on." Half stooping, apologetic; ready to sit down, waiting to be asked.

"Stay, stay," from my grandmother. Then: "Well? What's new? You looked? Anything good on tonight?"

"Pooh. Same old junk. Never nothing good."

TV is another prominent fact of life. They all watch television—what else is there? Their heroes are the teen-age idols of yesteryear. My grandmother loves loves loves Elvis Presley. (She probably imagines him in a *yarmulke,* with a shaved neck and earlocks. I'm only guessing.) The old folks observe the pop culture day by day—its soap operas, game shows, reruns, old movies; its commercials and more commercials. So they know all about us; you can't take them by surprise. After all, they don't have to make *sense* out of it; what is age for, if not to release you from such servitude? This is the modern world; anything goes; it's all in the script.

So my grandmother told me about a young woman she had seen while shopping at the A & P. The store was full of old-age pensioners of the neighborhood, timidly plucking their five-and-a-half-ounce tins of evaporated milk off the shelves, when in stomps this girl, briskly wheeling a cart and wearing—so far as I could make out, from the description—a cape, a nude body stocking and hip boots. That was it. Give her a mask, she'd be Batwoman.

"Everybody looked," my grandmother said. "But we didn't say nothing. We know it's the *style.*"

One of the things my grandmother likes about this place is that it is not "just for old people"; like public housing for the elderly—which would be a lot cheaper and cleaner, God knows. But she resents the category. I don't blame her. And she's right; this building, this neighborhood, are not just for the aged. That is not the lowest common denominator.

Uptown is the home of the displaced, the disinherited, the uprooted. What are called, these days, "internal immigrants." Appalachians, American Indians—aching with homesickness; the poor, the elderly, the halfway houses. They all find their way here by the same natural process, the end of the life cycle of a city neighborhood. That is why the bricks, cement, concrete pillars have the look of temporary shelters: tents, prefabs, lean-tos. Uptown is a D.P. camp; that is its secret.

So it is nothing to see people haggling with themselves in the streets, carrying on quarrels with unseen enemies, wheeling empty baby buggies, pawing through trash cans. They are more than old; they are outcast. They have escaped the net; they are outside every sort of social institution.

But why can't they come some other time, I would think— come when she's alone? She's alone so much. Why now? When I'm here. And—since it's no use if you don't tell the truth—who needs such visitors? Who wants them? I don't want to look at any more toothless mouths, black glasses, skinny arms, swollen livers. My grandmother is my grandmother—but who are they?

Which just goes to show: I didn't understand anything. Not the first thing.

My grandmother is one of the few in this building, in this whole neighborhood, for that matter—which is nothing but a vast reservation for the elderly—one of the very few who "has

143

anybody." Family, that is; who love and care; who don't just "pay visits"; who feel more than duty. And these others come to be close to that forgotten feeling. To steal up next to it, warm themselves at the fire. My grandmother knows this, and that's why she always tells me to "leave the door open for some air."

Ah, here's the rub. If that's true, if that's true—then what is she doing in a place like this? A place for those who have nobody? Who are alone in their extremity—forgotten, spewed up, swept out with the sawdust and ashes. The "wretched refuse," the "tempest-tossed." Refugees of old age, with their perishable goods.

Last winter the old lady tripped and fell in the house. Didn't we all tell her not to keep that crummy throw rug by her bed? She didn't break anything, but she was on the floor for seven hours, passing out, trying to pick herself up. Thinking of The Bobbe in the bathtub? I wonder. At her age, that didn't do her much good. It damaged her heart.

In the hospital, they doped her up; her mind wandered. I was afraid she would lose hold. Her lip curled back from the bright line of her teeth—a death snarl, a mummy. "Don't take any pills," I shrieked. "You know what pain is, you're used to it. Don't swallow anything; leave it under your tongue." Advice after her own heart; she's scared stiff of doctors, with their black bags, merchants of death. And hospitals: the smells, the sounds, the crack of light all night long under the door.

"You know how these old people are," the nurses kept saying, winking and tapping their foreheads.

All the old woman could think of was getting out, going home. She was still insisting, with a stubborn will—she could barely lift her head from the pillows—that she wasn't going to live with anyone.

But we all knew the time had come.

Everyone *offered*. Even I *offered*. She put up a fight. I live too

144

far from the rest; she'd be stranded out there, no one would come to see her. Besides, she knows I work at home and don't want someone looking over my shoulder. Her sons' wives are not Jewish, though that's not the real complication. "How come they don't visit me, if they want me so much?" Aunt Irene has an old mother of her own, paralyzed, in a nursing home in Quaker Pennsylvania. This other old woman was also looking forward—passionately: it was the only passion left— to going home. But they had auctioned off her house and all her belongings in the meantime. "Let Irene take care of her own mother instead."

As for the two gay, pretty daughters, with their busy social lives—my grandmother was ready with her defense. "You're never home. What would I do alone all day?"

"But you're alone all day now. Why do you want to give us an argument, Ma? You know you're no trouble."

What's the use of talking? You see what a stubborn old woman she is.

No one heard what she was saying. That she wants to be taken care of, she needs to be; she's too old, too weak, she's ready to lay her burden down. But what good is it, moving in with someone, if she's to be "no trouble"?

My mother would have taken her as a matter of course. She quit her job to take care of their father when he was dying. She's the one who does that sort of thing in our family. But my mother was about to go on a cruise. She had put down her deposit; she was looking forward. Ten days in the Caribbean, a call in Venezuela. All her friends go on cruises. The poor woman had her heart set on it. And she didn't see why one of the others, the rest of us, couldn't take care of my grandmother until she got back.

This was cruel. My mother didn't deserve to be put in this position, not after all her faithful service. But her father died fifteen years ago. She has since joined the Great American

Public. And she's fifteen years closer to the grave herself—that's what it's really all about. She has discovered that life is for having a good time—a recent discovery with her, as it is historically. Better late than never. Happiness has become a novelty item. Everyone's got to have it. Since when do the Lumpenproletariat take cruises to Venezuela? And the death of a child used to be an ordinary event. Now it seems terrible, the worst that can happen. Did it seem less terrible when it was common? I might ask my grandmother, who lost two of her own; but she's not talking.

After two days at Sylvia's, her husband said, loud enough for the old woman to overhear: "Why don't you put your mother in a Home, where she belongs?" Well, everyone knows how he is. He was raised in a Home himself, an orphan.

My grandmother couldn't wait until she crept back here, to her hole in the wall. A triumph of sorts. She heard the sigh of relief. Because she's so stubborn, so independent, she won't take anything, she won't become a burden to anyone. Because she's not senile—"Thank God"—and she never complains. Those seem to be the alternatives. It's nobody's fault. She knows it's *the style.*

So the subject was canceled; it will never come up again. She will live out her life here, stick it out to the end. It's too late to leave now. She has become attached to her belongings, her surroundings, her own stubborn independence—no matter how wretched. It's not for us to say. To her neighbors, tapping on doors with rubber-tipped canes. Checking up on each other, of course: they all have a fear of not being found for days. Roots? No time to talk of that. Barnacles, better. To cling or not to cling. She has found her last spar.

It's fiercer than ever now. If you go to the store for her, right away out comes the "pocketbook," her fingers prizing the clasp. "How much? Huh? How much?" Her big feet push her slippers across the floor, her hands drag the backs of the chairs. Her mouth is tight, as if she has suddenly thought of something she has forgotten to do. And her voice is getting rough; I find myself raising my own voice more and more. She peers round at the sound, turning her whole self stiffly sideways; an old white porcupine heavy with quills. She seems to be using all her senses at once, trying to make out a strange noise in the dark. Do you think she could be getting a little deaf in her old age?

HOW WE GOT THE OLD WOMAN TO GO

I'm coming into O'Hare at nine o'clock," I said.

"Why?" my mother said.

Some answer. I held the phone to my ear, feeling a little foolish. What do you mean, why. What kind of question is that. "Why not?"

Her voice was resonant; I thought she had been crying. I imagined tears blazed on her cheeks. It still scares me to hear my mother cry; the way it used to whenever she started talking Yiddish in front of me. I didn't understand and wasn't meant to. Something inside tightens its grip.

"And you want Daddy to pick you up, I suppose."

"Well, yes."

"Better tell me again, then. I have nothing to write it down with. I'm in bed with an awful bad cold."

Looked like no one was going to meet me at the airport.

My grandmother had died the night before; the funeral was tomorrow. I was in New York when my mother called with the news. "No one expects you. You don't need to come." Hard to tell what this meant; after all these years I still don't speak her language. "You have your memories," she said. I do? I thought, worried. I couldn't think of any memories. All I could think of were a lot of No Trespassing signs. PRIVATE. KEEP OUT. The woods were papered with them. The Past is not such a good neighbor. It knocks when it wants, but it won't let you in. What good are memories?

This wasn't exactly news. It had taken almost a year. It was spring when she fell and broke her hip—I was away then too —and by now it was the middle of December. So it was an old story; the same old story. Nothing was spared. Everything she had been afraid of, holding out with such will. All that was no good to her now—her own worst enemy. "She could last a long time." I couldn't see myself strolling in Central Park while they were putting the old woman into the ground.

150

"It's Bette, Ma. Bet-te Lee. She's been a-way. She came to see you."

My mother bent her dark cheek over the pillow and raised her voice coaxingly. The old woman's eyes were shuttling back and forth, back and forth, in her close-mouthed face. Since when was it so small? And white as spittle. Her hair was bound in a wispy topknot. I thought of shrunken heads with the lips sewn shut.

"Don't she look cute?" Roxy said. "We showt her a mirror, so she coult see how cute she lookt."

Up went my mother's head, straight as a rifle barrel. Loaded, of course. I gave her a swift kick under the bed.

"But she din't like it. Dit you, Bub?" She calls her mother-in-law "Bub" for short. They are *landsleit*, in a manner of speaking. My grandmother spent her girlhood in Kentucky, bluegrass country; Roxy is from the eastern hills. Even her face is hilly. A lean whittled jaw, the eyes close together and fanatical. A cigarette quivered between two crossed fingers. "You're too particular for an old lady, aincha?"

The old woman's eyes were busy busy.

Well, what did we expect. What ever made us think it was going to be easy. That one day she would just make up her mind, close up shop—lift her shoulders, bite off the thread. We all know how stubborn she is. Even now her head had a purchase on the pillow—like her hands on the sheets. Like her features on her face. Slanted back, steep, severe. Her brows were outthrust and her mouth was gripping. They would have to come and get her first. They would have to pry her loose.

Rudy came padding out of the bedroom, sliding his belt into his pants. He's on nights this month, he'd just got up. In fact, he had only one eye open, the other squeezed under his brow. It gave him a grousy look, frowning down at us—he has his mother's tufted brows—with one stinging eyeball. Rudy

151

doesn't talk much. He doesn't listen either. The floor was thudding under his bare feet.

"Here's Rooty. We're going to get you up now, Bub. Want to show Bette Lee how we get you up? First you neet your collar, don't you? She don't like it neither," Roxy said, dropping a glance over her shoulder, snapping the foam rubber neck brace in place. The short crop of her ponytail bounced with rough enthusiasm: "You don't like nothing no more, do ya?"

The fall had also dislocated a couple of vertebrae—though they didn't find out till later.

My grandmother had shut her eyes and fastened her lips, offering her chin on a chopping block, in a noose. Her lids were flickering. She looked both timid and aloof. Now she hooked up an eyebrow and stole a glance out of the side of her head at Rudy—standing in the window, his arms wrapped across his chest. An obstruction, a beam. His hair is so short it bristles and glistens. A breeze was rattling the paper shades.

"Oh. It's the *narr.*" Her lids sank shut. But her voice. Her voice. You could have blown it out. I felt something snuffed, extinguished.

I frowned at my mother. "Wha'd she call him?"

"You heard her. The *narr.* The fool. That's what she says, all the time now. Right to his face. It's the funniest thing." She put a finger to her lips. "But shhh. Don't say anything. It hurts his feelings something terrible."

When in Rome do as the Romans do.

Everyone knows that Rudy is his mother's favorite. No one begrudges him that. After all, what are a mother's feelings for, if not to make up for life's short rations? It's not just a preference, it's rapture; the undemonstrative old woman's joy in life. He was the child of her middle age. My grandfather used to blame it all on that.

He stood staring straight past us, over our heads.

Of course, it would be nothing for Rudy to lift his old mother. He weighs twice as much as she does—250 would be my guess—he's almost twice as tall. It's her tubes, her bags, her braces, her bruises, her bones. She's not sick; there's no disease. She's just broken. And she's no help, either. You can't tell if you hurt her. "She won't never complain."

Naturally. Not giving out her position to the Enemy.

Rudy hauled her up under the arms. Her mouth shrank; her chin poked over her collar; her elbows struck her sides. For a moment she looked like something hanging by the neck, swinging from a hook. Her big blue feet dangled and dragged; so much dead weight.

"Her feet," my mother cried. "What happened to her feet?"

I stuck her in the ribs, but not in time. She had picked up her head—her white trademark. The rubbed red spots stood out in her cheeks. "Her feet look burned. How did her feet get burned?"

Awkward silence. Roxy knelt by the wheelchair, slamming the footrests; clipping the catheter bag to the rail. Its dark tea was swishing and foaming. Her cigarette twitched in her tightened lips. Rudy clings to the hope she will die of lung cancer. "That's right. Uh huh. I burnt your mother. Dit it on purpose. That's the kint a care I take."

She looked like a teen-ager in her cut-off jeans, the little whip of hair switching on her neck. She stalked haughtily out of the room. Rudy stared.

"Now look what you done. She still ain't talkin to me from the last time." You've got to hand it to my mother; it's something to get a rise out of Rudy. His arms hung at his sides; his brows crouched in his face.

My grandmother had lowered her eyes; her lips were pressed together with firm intentions. She looked small, almost fugitive, perched over the wheels and spokes of the

153

chair. This is the way she always gets when angry voices are raised around her. "Just look down, don't say nothing." That's her motto. One she recommends to her children, with such results as you see. I was beginning to understand why she has resisted going to live with any of them all these years. Maybe it wasn't just pride—shame for her own condition. Maybe she was more ashamed for theirs.

"Your mother," Rudy said, looking at me over his shoulder, thrusting his way past. "Why don't you tell your mother?" Behind her back he suddenly turned, pushed out his face, and put out his pickled white tongue.

"What's that for?" As if I didn't know.

"So?" He shrugged, his hands spreading his pockets. "That's what the doctor used to do. The one that took care of Ma in the hospital."

"That's a big recommendation." Copycat.

"Why not? What do you want from them? They're human."

That's what you think. Please don't tell that to my mother. Doctors are her natural adversary. They hold the franchise on life and death. And who gave it to them? And whose side are they on? She has fallen into their hands.

My mother has powers of her own. I had just got back; everyone was waiting to jump on me. "Your mother. You know your mother. Better tell your mother." Right. Tell her. Go explain that she feels guilty about her mother's accident, her agonies—the fact that she isn't taking care of her herself —that that's what's eating her; that's why she finds fault with every little thing, her hand against every man's, won't let up for a minute. She believes she is battling for her mother's life. Tell her.

"Oh, Mother," I said.

"What's the matter? I'm not supposed to say anything?"

Her skin was the color of an autumn leaf; the dark slopes contrasted with her bold white hair. Holding her tongue? Yes, she was holding her tongue. Like a dog with its teeth sunk into your leg—that's how my mother holds her tongue. My heart was not in this. I knew what she was thinking. *And when it's my turn—when my time comes—who'll put up a fight for my sake?* Don't look at *me*.

The girls were sunning themselves on their elbows and stomachs on the back porch, portable radios fixed to their ears; waiting for Rudy to go to work. "What's taking him so long? Ain't he ever gonna get outta here?" The TV set was blaring in the living room; flies buzzed over the dishes in the sink. The little boy, Jordie, came stomping up the stairs—giving them a trouncing—soundly slamming the screen door. The other kids pick on him; he was fighting back tears. They seeped from under his big blurry glasses. He's like one of those foundlings his father is always bringing home. Home. Anyone can see Rudy has a soft spot; opinions differ as to where it might be.

From the glum bedroom, crammed with their two double beds, at right angles—there isn't room enough to turn around (their lives are separate, but not private)—we could hear Rudy's voice. Sullen, insulted. It always sounds that way. The voice of a deaf man. He's not that deaf. From Roxy ominous silence. Well, the old woman always liked a bit of life around her.

"The *narr*," she repeated, pinching her napkin under the hinge of her thumb. She was waiting for her dinner. Any day now.

My mother cocked her head at me. "Guess she knows something we don't know." Then her face changed. Her range was point-blank. "My God. How stupid can they be. Showing her a mirror."

In the kitchen a candle was smoking in a glass. *Yahrzeit*, in memory of my mother's father—the old woman's husband—who had died almost to the day, many years before. The little flame licked and lapped at the clear pool of wax. It reminded me not so much of the old man himself, may his soul rest in peace, as of the house I grew up in. The pantry was full of scorched glasses; we seemed so often to have them lighted in the kitchen, sputtering away. A gruesome effect; I knew what they were for. They cast such big shadows over the walls.

It was all a mistake. That's why no one met me at the airport. They thought I meant nine o'clock in the morning. "We wondered why you'd be coming in tomorrow morning."

She was in robe and slippers, her face shiny with cold cream, her straight cheeks shedding light; a crown or paper collar wound round her splendid white hair to keep its set for tomorrow. My mother is splendid—can she help it? A Noble Savage; a cigar-store Indian. About time I figured it out. But something was the matter with her mouth. It overshot the mark; puckered up like purse strings, an empty pouch. I keep trying to tell her that a bridge is not just for cosmetic purposes, but she can't wait to take her partial dentures out at night. On her little finger—her hands are large—she wears my discarded wedding band. Been helping yourself to my things again, huh? Finders keepers. Though it seems a weird choice of trinket—*memento mori.*

She intercepted my stare.

"Well, *you* didn't want it, *did* you?" She tugged her robe round her shoulders, her wide spreading bosom, and the rim of gold caught the light.

On the floor was a small neat pile of my grandmother's belongings they had given my mother at the nursing home. Half a dozen cotton nightgowns, laundered and folded; a pair of striped knitted slippers; a clear plastic brush whose lucid bristles reminded me forcefully of the old woman's hair. Oversized disposable diaper pads with blue plastic liners. It struck me as oddly like the collection you might take home from the hospital with a new baby. More like the beginning than the end of something.

"The End of an Era," as my father said. So people really say things like that.

He was stopping the clocks. Otherwise I would never get to sleep. He has all these clocks, chime clocks; they sound like a church mission. People break them and throw them away; my father finds them and fixes them. "Only a Little Something Wrong." They don't keep the same time; they are set to sound off one after another, so you can hear their voices, diagnose various frets and complaints. Your ear laid to the dark like a ticking chest. I say that walls Should Be Seen and Not Heard, as we were forever told as children. As you can see, my father loves slogans. "Might Makes Right." [*Sic*] "You Can Fool All of the People Some of the Time." "For Want of a Nail . . ." Why was he telling me all this? And I know for a fact he thinks this must mean I have a Bad Conscience. That is his opinion of a sleepless night. After all, he can sleep through anything; if he can sleep through his snoring. "Warm Feet, Cool Head" is his sure-fire formula.

He was reaching his big hand inside the glass cases remorsefully, as if he were robbing their nests. A scholar's specs, a prizefighter's nose—flattened, mutilated, like a statue's—eyes like cornflowers in a crannied wall. Years ago, when we lived in a house on the West Side, he would come up from tending furnace in the basement with his thick-clustered head whitened with sawdust and cobwebs; from scraping the pipes. That's the way it looks now.

"No visitation," my mother said. "Sylvia and I decided. We don't want. It's all a lot of 'Hi, how are you,' and 'I haven't seen you in such a long time.' Phoo. Is that what they call paying respects? Leon don't care, you know him; he leaves it up to us. But Rudy wanted. He says policemen always have visitation. Sure, they're Irish. Them and their wakes. How many Jews have they got on the force? And all Jews like Rudy, I bet. But I want to get there early tomorrow for Rudy's sake. That's when the police are coming. My poor kid brother. What else has he got? And besides, he goes to all of theirs."

"I'd like something of hers," I said. "I know there wasn't much, there wasn't anything. Just something that belonged to her. Something she touched."

My mother thought for a moment. Then she looked pleased. Over the candles her features lit—a struck match. "I know. Her clock."

A large blunt back rose in front of the room. It was Rudy, a black circle of a skullcap perched on his head. The back of it has more flesh than hair. He glanced over his shoulder—Oh, it's you—and lifted his arms across his chest. He was alone with the chairs and the long narrow blue box. It was open, the raised cover padded in Styrofoam, packing material. Inside— lying on wrappings and ruffles of starched stiffened gauze— was another box. This one was shut. A painted wooden lid. It was the figure of an old woman in a sunken blue bodice, with a bit of lace pinned to her transparent hair. Her eyes were stuck down, her mouth was fixed. Her glue had dried. I realized that this was supposed to be my grandmother. I realized that this was my grandmother.

"There," Roxy said, leaning down to the old woman's ear. It seemed to cling to the side of her head, her white nest, as in some chill wintry blast. "There. Now you got your bib on. Now you can show Bette Lee how nice you eat. She likes company to sit and watch her whilst she eats."

She does? She sure don't look it. Her head was clamped into her collar, a paper napkin bunched under her chin. Her stiff fingers plucked the spoon. But Roxy is the authority now, on

158

all my grandmother's likes and dislikes. Who would have thought the old woman had so many? I pulled up a chair and sat down close to the wheelchair. Too close. I was practically right on top of her. It was because my seat was so low—Jordie's, kiddie furniture. (I'd catch it for sure if he found out. Jordie is not only possessive, he's dogmatic. "It's not nice to . . ." "You must ne-ver . . ." He talks like one of Dickens's little orphans, his lip between his big ragged new front teeth.)

We were face to face, eye to eye. Our two heads were at the same level. I don't think this ever happened before. And I know she felt my gaze. A quick reckoning glance glimmered under her lids. My grandmother can't stand to have people watching her.

"Whatcha looking at? You?"

That's what she always says to me. "You-all? Whatcha looking at?" Clicking her tongue. She knows I get a kick out of her Kentucky Yiddish. What a combination. Clucking chiding cooing. A Jewish pigeon. "Go on. That girl. Always looking. She thinks she's gonna see something."

She said nothing now. She began to eat, silent and blinking. She seemed to have aged a hundred years. It wasn't any of the things I had been afraid of. No wrinkles, no trembling, no coarse threads on her chin. No munching lips. (She was blowing, cautiously, on her spoon.) None of the above. She just seemed covered with frost, like ice on a window. You could sense that her nerves took a dazzled concentration. All her movements were solemn and premeditated. Each time she took a bite, she gravely pressed the napkin to her lips—her fingertips brittle, pinching; starfish. Her lids grazed her cheeks. She was brushing my gaze like a fly off her face.

It was a new sensation. How often do you get to watch your grandmother eat? I've never even sat with her at the same table. That's a fact, if a strange one. What good is a fact without some strangeness? Even years ago, when we had dinner at her house almost every Friday night and always on holidays—especially then—my grandmother never sat down to eat with us. She carried hot pots from the kitchen, her apron hoisted, tied under her arms. I questioned this once.

Maybe it was a Passover Seder. At my father's house—my other grandparents—these ceremonies went on well past midnight, the old man singing and swinging his glass; until he himself suddenly fell asleep at the table, just like one of the children: his head laid on the wine-stained cloth, his two hands clapped under his cheek. He had a mustache like a bale of hay on his lip. After he died (and his wife followed within weeks) there was one more Seder on that side of the family. We sat down to the familiar table—the seltzer bottles, the blackened silver, my grandmother's dishes tinted the pink of the chambers of seashells; the sedimented wine, a sweet purple dye. We opened our books; the men felt their heads to straighten their caps. My uncles groaned, "Let's eat."

Here things fell somewhere in between these extremes. There was something hasty and droning about the whole business. Year after year they discussed what to leave out and what to leave in while my grandfather glowered over these territorial concessions. My father read Hebrew very deliberately—letter by letter—and the others were always after him to hurry, keep up, quit slowing them down. But he took his sweet time, rocking back and forth, his head smooth and shiny in his skullcap and his voice tolling out after the rest:

" . . . *minayim shekol mako umako.*"

" . . . *mako umako!*"

It even sounded like an echo, hollow, reverberating. You could tell he didn't really know what he was saying.

I finally piped up. "Where does *Bobbe* eat? How come she never eats with us?"

My sister Slim had already drunk all her wine—she always

did, first chance she got to tip up her glass—and now she was crabby, her cheeks flaming red, and my mother was holding her down on her lap with one hand, stuffing matzohs in her mouth to make her shut up, and turning the pages of her book with the other.

"And this one with the questions," my mother said, smacking me on the side of the head and shoving my face in the direction of my plate. That was her name for me. "This One."

"Not in the Head," my father said, in ringing tones. Even at the time, when I didn't know there was a word for it, I knew my father had principles.

"Look who's talking. The Big Shot," my mother said.

Words of Yiddish passed over the table like the Angel of Death. It was the language of bad news; bodily functions; the parts of dead chickens.

My grandfather brought his fist down on the cloth. Actually it was a bed sheet; who had tablecloths? He hated noise. Many was the time we seemed to leave the house rather suddenly, beat a hasty retreat, the way we would grab our blankets and towels and run from the beach when it started to rain. He was a large, impressive-looking man, broad jowls, broad shoulders, smooth iron hair. It had a solid luster, like the candlesticks. He rose, buttoning his jacket. He always wore a jacket and tie, not just on holidays. And there was something in his bulk, his hoisted shoulders, injured dignity, that makes me think of Rudy. He began to pronounce the names of the ten plagues of Egypt in a stern, almost angry voice. As much as to say, on both your houses. *"Dom . . . Tz'fardea . . ."* Vermin . . . frogs . . .

We lowered our eyes and dipped our fingers in the wine. Like I was saying, it was an embarrassing question.

The old woman dropped her eyes and blew on her spoon. She seemed almost to be counting to herself; almost a ritual. I looked and looked. I will not say to my heart's content. How could that be? I couldn't learn her by heart; she wasn't going to keep. I was looking so hard and so long that she was almost finished by the time I caught on to what she was doing. It was a can of stew Roxy had heated up for her. My grandmother was systematically spitting out the chunks of meat and storing them in her fist. Not kosher.

She thinks she's gonna see something.

All right for you. You and your secrets.

There was a commotion in front of the room. A group was approaching, all together—hanging, holding on to each other, pushing, crowding. They all seemed to be talking at once. They looked like a conga line. They stopped abruptly in front of the box. Their voices were tensely lowered.

"Ma! Don't cry. Ma! If you cry . . ."

It was Auntie Hodl and her family—my grandmother's youngest sister. Fat matronly Theda and her handsome husband; little Sherwin and his tall stylish wife; the wife's parents; and of course Hodl's husband. The old man was twisting his head and staring all about the chapel as they yanked him along. His cap was on crooked. The rest were staring at Hodl. She was the only one who was looking at the stiff horizontal features in the box. She seemed to be wearing half a dozen sweaters and her pants were stuffed into her boot tops. She resembled an old Chinese peasant with her smooth flat cheeks and slanted eyes. Now they were glittering. Her shoulders sagged; she let out a sigh.

"That's right, Ma. Keep it up. Just keep it up. After I told you—"

"How's she supposed to keep from crying?" I said.

"Doctor's orders," snapped Theda, without turning round —pushing out her face more threateningly at her mother. The old woman hung her head. She looked ashamed. "I got a bad heart, kiddo," she said.

She sat down beside me on the sofa, sobbing guiltily and popping little pills into her mouth. Her shoulders shuddered as if she had hiccups. The others piled into the next row, pulling the old man along—since he has to be propelled—and as soon as they sat down resumed staring hard at Lena. Theda, right behind her, pushed up her sleeves and folded her arms.

Of all The Bobbe's grandchildren, Theda is the one who takes after that remote ancestor—the old gypsy. I wonder how many millennia it took to make such features: the wide impassive cheekbones and half-hidden eyes. But something pained in her expression spoils it. My mother says it's because Theda was raised according to some dictatorial method of child rearing fashionable at the time. No matter how hard the infant cried, no matter how the mother's nipples squirted and ached, it couldn't be fed—couldn't even be picked up—until the hand saluted on the clock. And as a matter of fact she has the look of a hungry baby, her eyes squeezed up and her mouth squeezed down; her face and her forearms prominently displayed.

Hodl kept sneaking backward glances at her husband. His face was beaming, smooth as soap. Hodl shaves him. "Listen, dolly, do me a favor—fix his cap it shouldn't fall off." She doesn't know my name. "That's better," she said, biting her lip. She stuck her fist in her eye. "I wanted so bad to go and see her in the hospital."

Theda looked over. "You're starting in again? Fine. I'm going to march you straight home."

"And now they won't let me go to the cemetery."

"Ma! What did I tell you? There's nothing to see."

"Maybe we could take her," I said.

"No. She's not dressed warm enough. She hasn't got enough pills."

The funeral director was hanging around. "Oh, no, I wouldn't recommend that," he said, worried, rubbing his hands. His hair was as black as his paper skullcap. "No, not if she's not well. I wouldn't want to take such a responsibility."

"You see," Theda said.

Out of the corner of his mouth the funeral director addressed me. "Please, lady. I don't want no trouble. I got all the business I need."

A lot of people were coming by now. My mother turned up her face, tears streaming sideways across her cheeks like rain on a window. They closed the box. There was a hush. So it was time. I had a sinking feeling, a kind of stage fright. All right, old lady. You're on your own.

"Call your mother." That was the first thing my grandmother said to me when I came to her house. "Call your mother." She knew it was the last thing I wanted to do. There is something very peculiar about the relations between mothers and daughters these days. She wasn't criticizing exactly—just letting me know. My mother is a hard person to live with; she won't live with her herself. Still, it was an unnatural situation. No good could come of it. Maybe she knew someone would have to pay. Maybe she knew it would be her.

My mother called. My grandmother was at her house. Rudy had walked out on Roxanne. For a change; usually it's the other way around. "He didn't expect Ma to catch on, sick as she was. He never thought she'd take in what was going on. That's the part he couldn't stand. It was too humiliating."

I had to come north immediately, rent a "two-bedroom apartment" and "hire a woman" so I could take my grandmother off her hands. My mother has been after me for years to move to the North Side. She knew it was my intention to leave Chicago altogether. That was why she kept harping on a "two-bedroom apartment."

"Why do we have to go through all that? Why can't she just come here?"

"No. That's no good. The family wouldn't be able to see her. They'd be afraid to go out there—in that neighborhood." What did you think I had in mind? I wanted to take the old woman; I couldn't take the family. But that was a contradiction—how could you separate them? She stood for the family. She *was* the family. Rudy thought, if he had her in his house, she would make it a family too.

It was up to us; the others weren't even in the running. Sylvia said she "would love to have" her mother. But Fred had put his foot down. Fred can be counted on for that. Leon said she would be welcome to stay with him and Irene "if she could get up and go to the bathroom by herself." As if that wasn't the problem.

We didn't ask much, did we; we only asked her to *get better;* we only asked her to be *as before.*

Anyway, they were going to Europe. I guess they got fed up with looking at Fred's slides. "Europe," my grandmother sniffed when they told her. Her head sank scornfully into the pillow. "Europe. *I've* been there."

I felt my mother was trying to use her mother—to trap me, to get me in her power again. Make me part of the family. I knew she wasn't going to let the old woman come to me; she knew I wasn't about to go there.

"Mother. If that's the case. You have a two-bedroom apartment. Why can't you hire a woman?"

"I? How can I hire a woman? You have nothing better to do."

What business did the old woman have, living so long? Her own children were too old for this. Time was running out on them too. How did they know how much they had left? "She could last a long time." It was her life against theirs.

I had told my mother that I would move in with her and help her take care of my grandmother. I didn't remind her now and she didn't remind me. She felt trapped too by the old woman's lingering death. It was in our feelings for each other that we failed her.

It's strange. The city has been built up so much in the last few years, distances have shrunk in the grip of the expressways. But Jewish Waldheim seems as far out as it has always been. The same long bumpy ride, the car horns, the curtains drawn in the back of the black and silver-gray hearse. It still seems nowhere. A muddy brown pasture in the midst of factory fences, industrial waste. This is the new part, where the stones lie flat and they have something called "perpetual care." The mud was full of dried sticks of grass. I had forgotten that my mother's father is buried amongst my father's people. They were all around us, tarpaulins spread to protect the graves. All the same, a lot of mud was getting dug up and tracked. The ground was just iced over; glazed puddles. I went to stand behind my mother's chair.

Her cold was bad and she was all bundled up—like Hodl: boots, pants, sweaters, scarves. The more she had put on, the smaller she looked; stooping. She seemed to shrink before my very eyes. Now, when she felt my hand on her shoulder, she turned herself sideways to see who it was, her head poking forward as if she had a stiff neck; her cheeks bound in a babushka. It scares me how much she is getting to look like my grandmother. *Listen, Mother, don't do this to me. I'm not ready for it yet.* She reached up a mittened hand.

It seemed strange to me that my grandmother was at one and the same time carrion—garbage—that had to be got rid of, shoveled quickly out of sight; and something precious and tender, of infinite value, being laid away as if for safekeeping —sunk in a vault. These things seemed opposed, but they weren't; they couldn't be; because both were true. It was necessary to hold them both in your mind at once. That's all we were trying to do, standing over the open grave.

166

But it was very cold. You could see the rabbi's breath puffing in front of his beard. He was young, and the hairs spread brightly and ripely over his chest and almost up to his eyes. In the chapel, as soon as he had opened his mouth, I knew it was going to be all right. He wasn't going to talk like Dylan Thomas. And he was no sadist—he was making it quick. Of course, it would have been nice to prolong the services. A shame to waste such an opportunity. A raw windy day, a low sky, a box suspended over the straight steep sides; pinched faces somberly staring. Funerals are the only chance you get. Weddings and bar mitzvahs are practically useless. Happy occasions; people are thinking of the presents. At weddings they all want to write their own scripts anyway; be original; make up new words. For funerals the old words seem good enough.

But it was just too cold. The wind was goading. People couldn't stand still. Humiliating to be thinking about your fingers and toes when you knew your mind ought to be on eternity. The sky was as white as the trail of a jet.

Two workmen bent, releasing the tapes. The long blue box slid smoothly downward. I felt my grip on my own life loosen a little.

The four surviving children rose to say *Kaddish*. Fred, Sylvia's husband, standing behind her, lifted his head, a keen look in his eye, reciting the words with firm conviction.

"Yisgadal v'yisgadash shma rebo . . ."

It startled me a little. Fred is an orphan, the lucky dog; his parents died when he was small and a large family of brothers and sisters grew up in "The Home." This sounded like a good setup; I would have been willing to take my chances. But people talked as if it was something catching: "He's from The Home." "He got that way in The Home." His children to this day correct his pronunciation:

"Daddy. It. Doesn't. Mean. An-y-thing."

167

"That's like I say. It don't mean nuttin."

A sly foxy glance, a sharp chin, shrewd lifting brows. White cotton pads of sideburns. His hands in fur gloves clasped to the front of his coat. For reasons of her own, my grandmother always called him by his last name, Solomon. She never called him Fred. He was her son-in-law thirty-five years. It was still *Solomon*. And if the world ended tomorrow, it would still be *Solomon*. She never said a word against him—she didn't need to. Everyone knew what she meant. We all pretended not to notice anything amiss.

Uncle Leon was knocking back and forth, rocking on his toes, just like the bearded old Jews in *shul*. Tall, bushy-browed, ermine-haired—a kind of smooth thick white fur slicked sidewise over his temples. He is the one who takes after his mother; it's not just the features, it's the expression. He looks as if he's keeping his thoughts—the best ones—to himself. I remember him once, when I was small, frowning down at me, shaking his head and wondering out loud: "What *good* are girls? What *good* are girls?" Now he was mumbling and ducking his head; it hung forward, red-, shame-faced. His lips shuffling mechanically. "Na na na na." It was nonsense syllables. He was only making off; imitating the fervent old men with their chanting and swaying.

Roxy and the kids were standing behind Rudy, looking at his coat. The girls with stung sullen faces, shrinking and shivering in leather jackets, hiding their fingers up their sleeves. The little boy, his glasses like a pair of obstacles, peering out from under them in his elderly way. Lost. Where does he come from? They're a bunch of giants and he's such a peanut. And Roxy, somber and striking in black, all six feet of her, her legs elegant in black stocking, a veil loose about her cheeks. She was entitled. She was the one who had done what needed to be done.

Rudy was standing stock still, staring straight ahead with his unfocused, unflinching expression. As if he could feel their eyes on him. His hands were behind his back. His lips were not moving. So my father was right after all. This was it. The end of the line. It was all over. The old woman's sons were not going to say *Kaddish* for her. They didn't know how.

"Sarah? Sarah?"

The lab technician smiled and clutched her clipboard to her hip. "How are *you* today, Sarah?" A smooth blond head, big smooth white teeth.

My grandmother was lying on her side, on her cheek, a handful of hair gathered to the top of her head like a scanty white beard. Her large hands clutched the sheets. Her lower lip gripped the upper; a tube was fluttering in her nostril. One eye turned inward, sunk in its socket. The other stared.

"Don't you remember me? Sarah? Don't you know who I am?"

The girl bent down, encouraging; her voice got higher. "Do you know what time it is? Do you know what day it is? Sarah?"

The old woman's lip kept gripping. Her shoulder was lifted to her ear as if she expected to hear a terrible crash.

The girl stood up. A row of ballpoint pens was clipped to the pocket of her lab coat. "How long has she been like this?"

"Like what?" We all said it at once. We all turned on her.

"Like this." She shrugged. "Senile."

"My mother is not senile," my mother said. "My mother was never senile. She's sharp as a tack, sharper than any of us. You don't know my mother."

"It's only since the accident," Rudy said.

"What kind of accident? Even after the accident. After waiting three hours for an ambulance. Sitting on an orange crate in the storeroom at the A & P. Barefoot—her shoes flew off —that's how hard she fell. And then the doctor has the nerve to tell me—"

"Let's not get started on that now, Mother," I said. You keep flaying yourself like this, there won't be anything left for the knacker.

"She couldn't. 'She couldn't—not with that hip.' That's what he said. I saw it with my own eyes, and he's telling me. 'She couldn't have been conscious. She couldn't have been sitting.' Well, they don't know my mother."

How often she must have gone over it in her mind. Even the words hurt. Crash. Smash. Hip. Splinter. Smithereens. A bottle of cooking oil got knocked off the shelf and shattered in the aisle at the grocery. They picked up the pieces but the floor was still slick. You could say it was bound to happen, what with all the old people shopping there, in that miserable dregs of a neighborhood. Someone was bound to slip and fall. Maybe even break something. What fragile vessels we put our feelings in.

For some reason, after all that had happened, all that had gone wrong with the doctors, the hospitals—and everything had gone wrong; I'm not going to make a list: who doesn't know, who hasn't felt, the arrogance, the indifference, the shameful neglect; everything gains in value with age but a human life—of all there was to torment herself with, this had made the strongest impression on my mother. This was what stood out in her mind. *They don't know my mother.*

And it is the sorest spot. It is the hardest thing to take. They don't know. They don't want to know. And now of course they will never know.

The girl stood with her clipboard under her arm and her pens on her chest. "She doesn't answer my questions."

"Why should she?" Rudy said. "They're dumb questions."

He was standing at the foot of the bed, legs straddled, hugging his elbows in his blue uniform. His cheeks heavy, inert—as if he had a helmet strapped under his chin. I see what it is. He always looks on duty. "You think after all she's been through she cares *what day* it is? She'll think you're making fun of her, you ask her *what day* it is."

"But she has to care. You should talk to her. Orient her to reality."

"Oh, reality," Rudy said, with a deliberate, dumfounded grin—jerking his head up and down and showing his jack-o'-lantern teeth. "Hah. Uh huh. I see. Reality."

Die with dignity. Die with dignity. I know what it means. It means without all this. Without the doctors, the hospitals, the tubes, the technicians—why are they still squeezing blood out of this turnip?—without the TV set tilting down from the top of the wall with no one watching and the lights and buzzers that no one can reach. I know what it means. But what if dignity is not our lot?

The old woman lay on her side, in her crib, the tube in her nose and her face to the wall. *Hear no evil See no evil Speak no evil* Her skin was not so much wrinkled as twisted—wrung out. Her eye was sunk in its tunnel, her mouth clenched. She did not express apathy. She looked tenacious. She was hanging, holding on to something. Her lip. It was cracked and bleeding from the dryness of force-feeding. She had been hiding it from us the whole time: the lower lip defending it like a weapon.

A few days later Fred and Sylvia were sitting beside her bed for a long time. At last Fred got up and reached for his coat. "Come on, Syl," he said, raising his voice and pushing his arm into his sleeve. "We might as well go if she ain't gonna talk to us."

171

It would be *Solomon* who finally broke her silence. *Solomon* had always got her goat. The old woman lifted an eyebrow and rolled up an eye:

"What's there to say?"

"Just a little, three times," someone said behind me. The funeral director. Still hanging around. The nervous type. "Just a little, three times," the rabbi said. I struck the shovel at the pile of dirt. The earth was shockingly hard. The impact jarred me. It was all I could do to scrape up a few stones and scatter them on top of the lid.

The bulldozer bumped forward, gave a nudge; the whole pile slid and dumped in at once. Rudy ducked his head between his shoulders, stretching his neck out as if there might be more to see. His coat seemed too short for him, flapping at his knees. A good two inches of white sock showed at his ankle. It's not that his head is so small—it's that the rest of him is so big. He moved off, his hands digging his pockets, flicking a glance at Fred and me. Just a habit, professional; he didn't really see us. His back stiffened in the wind. I just realized; Rudy had lost his only friend. Nothing stands between him and his life. Only himself; a great sea wall.

We looked and looked. Everyone else had hurried back to the cars; they were closing the curtained doors of the hearse. But Fred seemed reluctant to go, hesitating, his chin pressed to his chest; his fur gloves laid one atop the other against his coat. "She always called me Solomon," he confided—shyly, not looking me in the eye. Glancing about under his mobile brows as if someone might overhear. "If she would of just once of called me Fred."

My father's two sisters and his brother were almost the last to leave—parked at some distance, making their slow way over the mud. They are heavy people and it was heavy going.

Aunt Dee in her cloth coat and Aunt Flor in her fur; their purses trailing by the handles at their sides. They seemed to be laboring slavishly under the law of gravity. It was obvious when I caught up with them that they had been talking— conversation stopped dead. I asked for a ride.

Once, many years ago, I happened to see Uncle Arnie standing on our front porch sticking a note in the mailbox. It was a summer evening; the screen door was on the hook. I went and peered out. He was the baby of the family, his face still lumpy and purplish with acne. He brought it close. "Tell Sammy his father died," he said, and ran down the stairs. His face is still lumpy and purplish, and whenever the family gets together he wants to know where all the good times went.

We stood beside the car, silently scraping barnyard mud from our shoes.

"Your mother," Aunt Dee said, turning on me. Her face was very close, puffy and pouchy, her teeth small and crowded. She looked like a chipmunk. There were creases under her eyes. I'm going to have that, I thought; I saw it in the mirror. Well well well; the rough with the smooth. Her eyes under her glasses were just like my father's—the same amazed blue specimens.

"Your mother."

As I have said, my mother's parents are buried in my father's family plot. There is a large stone bearing the name. Of course, today, there had been a lot of traffic; in spite of the tarps the mud had been trampled and churned on the graves. They were upset. "Showing no respect for the dead."

"What's my mother got to do with it? It's not her fault if the cemetery's getting crowded."

"She wanted those plots. She insisted. I didn't want to give. But you know your mother. It's her own way or nothing."

Usually it's nothing. Aunt Flor looked embarrassed; Arnie looked away. Aunt Dee has been a widow many years; twenty,

to be exact; it was a day much like this, a long drive to Waldheim, the air white with snow flurries. Her husband did not
leave her in good circumstances. He couldn't bear leaving that
way; had hung on long after the doctors had given up on him,
pedaling a Good Humor wagon with a face that must have
given his customers pause. I was not about to forget. Only—
one at a time, please. To tell the truth, just at the moment,
stepping on graves did not seem to me the worst thing in the
world. Not even the most inconsiderate. It didn't seem to
occur to them that they were "showing no respect for the
dead."

The workmen were still banging down the backs of their
shovels, flattening the earth on the top of her grave.

It was business as usual, the quarrels of the living. My
mother has a reputation for going where she is not wanted.
But why did she have to stick her poor parents where they
were not wanted? Wasn't the plot in the old cemetery good
enough? So what if it was all used up? That never made any
difference before. They're all buried on top of each other
there anyhow; especially the children, two or three in a grave.
Headstones and weeds all over the place. My grandmother's
family. They were always thick as thieves.

Rosie's husband Herschel was a fruit peddler, a little red-
faced man with hard cheeks polished like apples and tiny eyes
that seemed to be wincing and snapping with satisfaction. As
if he'd just downed a *schnapps.* Ahhh. He often stopped at our
house to take a glass of tea. His clothes stank to high heaven
and the fruit flies buzzed round him. His horse, Buck Jones,
was madly in love with its master. (It was named for a cowboy
star who perished in the Cocoanut Grove fire. All Herschel's
children were named for stars, cowboys and sirens.) Buck
Jones was blond, blunt-featured, with a white mane combed
to one side and bangs hanging over its brow. Rudy loved to

feed it apples he stole from the cart, just to see the creature swallowing them down whole—gulping them like yawns. Patient in its blinkers, flies scaling its lashes. Lifting up one hoof at a time. But when it felt that a sufficient interval had elapsed, Buck Jones would come climbing up the front steps, clipping and clopping and dragging the cart. Scales tipping, brown bags flying; rotten apples rolling in the street.

They say Rosie nagged Herschel to death. He got his revenge. All thirteen children looked like him. My mother told me he didn't just kiss the babies—he licked them; dragged his tongue over their faces like a cat. Rosie was something of a battle-ax, with her bowed legs and straight hair and a set of false teeth which looked as if they had been made for Buck Jones. She was always getting up packages to send to "the poor people." Naturally we all wondered who these poor people could be—with such a benefactor—and where she ever found what to put in her packages. Same place Herschel found his apples.

There are only three sisters left of all that tribe. Rosie is a cripple in California; Yetta has taken to her bed—not to rise and shine again, I fear. Hodl was the only one who could come to the funeral. And I couldn't get over her family—scolding the old woman, staring at her like a prisoner in a box. I happen to know that she baby-sits for them, often weeks at a time; takes care of their houses, their children, their pets—she hates pets—with her sick husband and her bad heart. (What's the matter with the in-laws, I'd like to know. They look to be in pretty good shape.) And now all of a sudden they were so worried about her they couldn't take their eyes off her for a minute. Of course they were worried; they were scared stiff. People have a funny way of showing these things.

It was time. Funerals are the last outpost of family life—the last stronghold of such feelings. That is why they bring out such strange behavior. My father's family, like Hodl's, were simply trying to express their sense of what was fitting to such an occasion. A public statement of continuity, solidarity. At the same time you could see they had their doubts; the most nagging suspicions. Their sacrifices were ready. But where was the altar?

"You have no regrets," Flor said to me as we were riding once more past dreary streets. "You went every day, every day." I felt as if she had slapped me in the face. What kind of person has "no regrets"? And who went "every day, every day"? I had plenty of regrets. And yet I was drawn to my grandmother—pulled to her. It wasn't a feeling. It was a force. The raw material of feeling. It was what had brought me back for the funeral. Surely it was worth something. Surely it was more powerful than these petty family differences. I knew I didn't have anything "better to do."

The family was sitting at Sylvia's. ("She keeps telling me, 'Tell people not to come, tell people not to come.' What did she want it at her house for, if she doesn't want people to come?") Fred belongs to the Skokie chapter of the Jewish Legionnaires, and in the evening they sent a *minyan*. The men arrived all at once, stood stamping in the doorway in earmuffs and galoshes, blowing on their hands, opening boxes musty with odors of prayerbooks and fringed prayer shawls. One had brought his son, evidently just bar mitzvahed—a pale boy in an embroidered cap. He looked scared to find himself in the House of Death, with its baskets of waxy-looking fruit, the thick yellow sponge cakes, the sheeted mirrors. He stared at all the people wearing their ordinary faces.

They chased the women out of the room. What *good* are girls?

Sylvia wanted to show off her new couches in the den. It seems that Mindy and her husband had gone on vacation and left their cats with her; and the cats had clawed up the furniture. "It's all right," Sylvia said cheerfully. "I wanted to get new." Sylvia is good-natured. I think it's called happy. Not to say complacent. But she and Fred dote on their things; what they throw out is as good as new. Even Gary's toys, when they gave them to my sons; as if he had never played with them. Years ago, when they lived with us, it was a wonder to me to see Fred carefully hanging up his clothes (no one in our house ever hung anything up), brushing them out, sticking his shoes on shoe trees. Something else he must have picked up in "The Home." It used to make me feel guilty whenever we came to their house, tracking in dirt—they watch your feet when you walk in the door; they say hello but they keep eying your shoes —throwing our coats on their bed, all bolsters and dust ruffles; using the little guest towels displayed in the bathroom. (I could never feel quite sure they were meant for me.) And that's the way it was now, as we all packed into the den and shut the door, taking our seats on the couches and folding chairs labeled "Weinstein & Sons."

A funny thing—some of the women were talking—the same thing had happened to them. Their children had gone on vacation, left them their cats, the cats had damaged the furniture. And they didn't even like cats. Couldn't stand cats. Who wants cats?

"Cats," Sylvia said. "That's what I get. Cats."

She stuck her fingers in the crooks of her elbows and looked at Mindy out of the corner of her eye. Voices rose against the wall; the men in the next room had started their prayers.

It was as if a gavel had been rapped—a meeting called to order. Sylvia had thrown the subject open to discussion. She was asking for agreement, for sympathy—almost, for justice. All the mothers were murmuring indignantly. They had a common protest. Their daughters were having cats instead of children.

Sylvia takes her mother's advice—she doesn't raise her voice, she drops her eyes. My grandmother used to hold her up to my mother as an example. Fred had the reputation of "making remarks" and "talking dirty," and in a family where the father always put on a clean shirt before he sat down to the table—and the mother never sat down to the table at all —you could see where that would go over big. So I could tell when Fred had said something; the blood would stand still in Sylvia's cheeks and her eyes would drop so quickly they seemed to clatter. These days she just glances down, briefly— the way she flutters her eyes over the rims of her Ben Franklin specs. And in a pretty matron, with a stunning silver tiara of hair, it's very effective.

It just so happened that all the Mothers had sat down on one side of the room, the Daughters on the other. So it was a kind of mock tribunal, a kangaroo court. The Mothers were bringing a case against the Daughters. There were about fifteen or twenty of us altogether, and except for Mindy and me, and Fern—Sylvia's new daughter-in-law, Gary's bride—the Daughters were not necessarily Daughters of these Mothers. That was all to the good. There is safety in numbers. The condition was generic; the complaint was general. The Mothers crossed their arms and stared. The Daughters stood accused.

"No children and no plans for any," Sylvia pronounced. "So they tell me." Looking from Mindy to Fern as much as to say, Well? What have you got to say for yourselves? Hmm? Why are you holding out on us? Where are our grandchildren?

Mindy was also looking down. You could see they had been through this before. Petite, almost breakable; her pliant hair hanging past her cheeks. Her face is so small—wedge-shaped —the cheekbones seem too big for it. But that is her beauty, the bit of strangeness. She gets the cheekbones from our

178

grandmother. And I was just noticing: her nose, delicately arched, is like the old woman's too. An exact replica. I know, because I had been studying another replica of my grandmother—the still features in the box—that very day. I didn't expect to see them ever again. And now here they were. We are her connection with the future.

You could picture the men swaying to their vibrating voices. The Daughters said nothing. They had already spoken. What better way to tell your mother what you think of her than not to have children? That was what they had to say for themselves. Their silence was accusing. You could feel the weight of hostility shifting. They didn't need to state their case against the Mothers. They had stated it so many times before.

Once again, the Mothers were to blame. Once again, it was all their fault. The burden of proof was on them; they were caught in the middle. Why not? It was a position they were used to. Has there ever been a generation more in the middle? They must have been sick and tired of rendezvousing with destiny. It seemed they had always been middle-aged; between their parents who had belonged to the old world and their children who didn't want to grow up.

Well, to give you have to have. They were the generation that "didn't know any better." Someone actually said that now. "We didn't know any better." (Who was talking about *knowing?* What did that have to do with it?) The Mothers—once again—were defending themselves.

"It was the psychology courses," Sylvia said. "That's what did it. We drove Gary to Champaign in September, and when we picked him up in December for Christmas vacation, he told us everything we did wrong."

"When you love a man, don't you want something from him?" Irene asked. She sounded worried.

"Children are just an extension of yourself," Fern said. "That's all. That's just as selfish." I guess she felt obliged to

179

say something because she is a Daughter-in-Law. She's even tinier than Mindy, hips smooth in French-cut jeans. Thirty; older than Gary—who doesn't look very old, alas, in spite of his mustache and muttonchops, his baby features swamped in corporate hair. Between the two of them they are now earning $45,000 a year. Every time I see Fred and Sylvia it goes up. Nothing else is new. At first Sylvia was proud. Now she seems puzzled. What do they want it for, if not "for the children"?

There were a lot of spent bullets whining around the room.

I heard my father's voice rasping after the rest. At the cemetery when they said *Kaddish* he took off his glasses. His eyes looked smaller, weaker, unused to the light; the big sunburned nose emerging between. His skullcap trimmed with curly gray hair. He seemed to be peering over a fence, a wall.

The men were tending to their business; we were holding a little post-mortem of our own. Because now—and everyone must have known this was coming—someone brought up a recent public opinion survey. It had run in a nationally syndicated advice column.

If you had it all to do over again, would you have children?

Eighty percent of the readers who wrote in in response answered *No.*

It's no use saying, So what, what does it prove, who cares about advice columns? My family are the readers of advice columns. And it's no use observing—as I was about to—that people who write in to advice columns are troubled souls, complainers to begin with—"Just a Bunch of Bellyachers," as my father would say. Because the same grievance was lodged in their hearts.

Now they tell us.

It was a revelation. It explained the whole thing. Explained it more completely than anything else could. They, themselves, had never wanted children. They should never have had Daughters in the first place. No wonder it had all been so difficult. They had been bilked, conned, hoodwinked, swindled, sold a bill of goods. (Hadn't they always said they "didn't know any better"?) Now they saw what the Daughters were saying. The Daughters wanted just what the Mothers wanted out of life. Only they wanted more. And they wanted it now. And they knew how to get it. They weren't going to run the race for happiness in any three-legged sack. No, thank you.

The Mothers stared. Once again the hostility shifted. Only there wasn't time; it was too late even for that. They didn't have it all to do over again.

My mother and I were not taking part in this discussion. My parents have five grandsons, not a bad hand to draw when you've started out—as they seem to see it—with a lousy low pair. She was standing pat. It cannot have been a very familiar sensation. For once she had nothing to reproach me with. For once life had not handed her a rain check.

She was lying on the sofa, a blanket on her knees, a pillow behind her back. Her cold was bad; she kept dipping her nose into a fistful of Kleenex. I couldn't help thinking: There she goes again—the couch and the Kleenex. But I knew this was real. Even her hair was limp. Her beautiful hair. The set hadn't held; it's getting too fine—or too thin. Getting that blown-dandelion look. You can see the pink scalp through the fibers. Soon it will be levitating.

From time to time we exchanged small smiles—a glance of complicity. We are veterans of these wars, battle-scarred. We've fought over this ground so many times before. We've been at it so long we've almost forgotten by now what the fighting was all about. We were practically comrades in arms. It was a kind of truce. No whistles blowing, no white flags waving. But it had suddenly dawned on me: my statute of limitations had just run out. The old woman is dead. My own children are grown. Soon I will be forty. Move over, Mother. I'm in the middle now.

In the next room strangers had finished chanting prayers for our dead.

And now I see that this squalid little tale is a love story. Is it our fault that this is the way love shows itself—hides its face —and that these are the remnants of our rituals? Everyone said it was a bad end. She didn't *die with dignity.* I'm not so sure. For us, yes—we were weighed and found wanting. I was heartbroken for her suffering, her humiliation, which seemed so undeserved—as if that's any criterion. It was bitter to know we had let her down. Maybe bitterest of all to guess what it meant. But she outwitted us; she kept her secrets. She went out on her own terms; even to the end she would rather have had us believe that she didn't know us, she was losing her memory, than let on how truly defenseless she was. And she didn't ask for anything; she didn't take. She was always so afraid of taking. You'd think someone was giving.

After the small settlement with the A & P for medical bills —they sent back her shoes—there was just enough from her savings left over to cover the cost of her funeral.

The clocks were ticking. My mother in her reading glasses was looking up a number in the telephone book, licking her finger as she lapped up the pages. Usually when I'm around she asks me to do this for her; but I was just getting ready to leave, going back to New York. As usual I had deposited some of my junk in her closets.

"Aren't you going to take anything with you?" she asked, glancing up, rather resigned, her cheek moving up and down in her hand. (My God. Doesn't it ever end? Don't we ever get rid of them? Don't they ever grow up?) The glasses, I suspect, are from Woolworth's. Their depths are serene, a thick diffused light. They seem to smooth and calm the Great Plains of her face. They accomplish something I have never been able to, imaginatively. And I don't think old age will do the job, either.

My father was honking the horn outside. Tapping it—the S.O.S. signal. He thinks he's the only man in the world who honks a horn that way.

My mother spoke quickly: "I can't tell you how glad I am you came," she said.

I know. That's what I came for. That's what this has been about.

I bent down with my bundles to give her a kiss goodbye.

"My cold, my cold. Don't catch my cold," she warned, lifting her face. It was suddenly luminous, her glasses brimming over with tranquil light. I can't live within ten miles of her; I dread the distance there must one day be between us. "I won't," I promised. So we turned our faces aside; our cheeks just touched. And we parted—yet one more time—forever.